THE ART
OF THE
ARROW

THE ART OF THE ARROW

HOW LEADERS FLY

Nick Christelis

publishing

2016

First published in 2016

ISBN: 978-1-86922-572-8
eISBN: 978-1-86922-573-5 (PDF eBook)

Published by KR Publishing
P O Box 3954
Randburg
2125
Republic of South Africa

Tel: (011) 706-6009
Fax: (011) 706-1127
E-mail: orders@knowres.co.za
Website: www.kr.co.za

Printed and bound: Creda, Eliot Avenue, Epping II, Cape Town, 7460, www.creda.co.za
Typesetting, layout and design: Cia Joubert, cia@knowres.co.za
Cover design and art work: Five0Six, info@five0six.co.za
Editing and proofreading: Jennifer Renton, jenniferrenton@live.co.za
Project management: Cia Joubert, cia@knowres.co.za

Endorsements

Nick's guidance has been indispensable to our business and has led to many breakthroughs and much of the innovation that we pride ourselves on. Nick knows better than anyone that we can all be leaders and this book shows us how. It is essential reading for anyone looking to grow and develop themselves, their team or business. It's a must read!

Yusuf Abramjee – Head of News and Current Affairs, Primedia Broadcasting and Lead SA activist

Nick, my 'Mr Miyagi' of leadership, has hit the target in the Art of the arrow: How leaders fly *by capturing the very essence of what it takes to be a great leader. An outstanding read with years of invaluable experience rolled into just over 200 pages.*

Adrian Goslett – CEO: RE/MAX of Southern Africa

It was such an awesome 'experience' going through chapter after chapter and almost reliving everything that you have taught me and my team at RICH about leadership over the years. Thank you for pulling everything together into one place – a great reference guide and/or reminder that we can go back to over and over again. The real life examples throughout the book really help to put the information in context, and provide real take away value to the reader. Anyone reading this book will find it an easy and extremely worthwhile read with simple to remember and valuable lessons.

Elizabeth Kobilski – CEO: Rich Products Corporation of South Africa

Wow! What a book! It is easy to read and flows nicely from one part to the next. I love the balance between professional and personal experiences that you have brought into the book to demonstrate leadership principles. What I found useful is that you relate past and present events – social, business, political and personal – in a simple but impactful way. I am sure the book will benefit new and experienced leaders.

Dan Moyane – Corporate Affairs Executive: MMI Holdings Limited; News anchor: eNCA

Nick Christelis has been my mentor for years, always encouraging me to push my professional boundaries and achieve more than I thought I was capable of. This book is a must-read for all those wanting to advance in their careers and be inspired by Nick's many professional adventures. Nick's unique story-telling ability will stay with you long after you've put the book down. I've always considered Nick to be my "Leadership Guru" and know you will too.

Katy Katopodis – Editor-in-chief: Eyewitness News

There is no better business school than the learning derived from the real business world. Over the years of interfacing with and consulting to CEO's across the globe, Nick has obtained an in-depth and thorough insight into the dynamic of leadership.

He understands how the leader can cultivate an innovative successful business to grow exponentially and has also witnessed some leaders who merely plod on with no real focus!

I have been privileged to have worked with Nick during my years at Famous Brands. His mentoring and advice has at times been tough, but always valuable – he says it like it is but always guides you to take that quantum leap!

This book captures years of leadership expertise and knowledge, delivered in a practical way.

Val Nichas – VBN Consultants

Dedication

For my wife, my children and my grandchildren.
"You are the wind beneath my wings"

Table of contents

About the author

Nick Christelis is the Managing Partner of Nick Christelis & Associates, a consultancy specialising in Aligning Execution with Strategy. With over 30 years of global consulting, he has developed a reputation as a business strategist, facilitator, coach and speaker.

As a coach, Nick has assisted many CEOs and their executive teams, and is regarded as a mentor by a number of SA's best-known and most successful business leaders. He has also coached many of SA's top sports people and teams on the psychological aspect of human performance.

Nick's strengths lie in his practical business experience, having been a director of numerous client companies as well as his ability to remain at the cutting edge of worldwide development in strategy and leadership.

Nick can be contacted at:

Nick Christelis & Associates
Email: nick@ncanda.co.za
Twitter: https://twitter.com/leadingguru
Website: www.NickChristelis.com

Preface by Steve Griessel

To say that Nick has had a big impact on my life and the lives of my colleagues is an understatement. Nick has been deeply involved in three organisations I have led, and all three times has been an integral part of our success.

During my tenure as Managing Director (President) of RCI Southern Africa, Nick worked with our team on two major initiatives over several years. The first was to instil the culture of our company at every level of the organisation so that it became a way of life.

The second was a continuous process of mentoring senior management into a strong unit that permitted people to utilise their talents fully in an open and driven environment.

When I became CEO of The Tourism Investment Corporation (Tourvest), a company which we listed on the Johannesburg Stock Exchange in 1998, I immediately invited Nick to become a core part of our team. Nick spent a substantial part of his time over the next four years working in a highly complex environment which quickly grew to 43 companies in various industries. His work ensured that everyone had a sense of purpose and the whole. He continually broke down barriers to communication, and at the same time helped us create a culture of constant learning and accountability.

After my family and I moved to the USA, I became the CEO of American Community Properties Trust, a diversified real estate firm with over 50 years of history, listed on the NYSE. The company owned and operated over 6,000 rental apartments and also owned more than 12,000 acres of land in St. Charles, Maryland, that we were developing into a beautiful community.

The company was facing the spectre of the financial crisis during 2008 and 2009 and much of the debt owed to banks was not going to be renewed. The management team and board of directors were faced with a complex turnaround situation needing quick and decisive action with no room for error.

In order to achieve this, with Nick's help, we utilised the holistic approach that he had mentored me on over the years. This encompassed a new vision statement; facing the brutal reality; setting clear strategy, goals and actions; holding everyone accountable; building trust; and changing the reward system to face the new reality. We were not only able to avoid a potential disaster, but completely remade the organisation and created significant shareholder value.

Nick's ability to grasp what needs to be done and have the flexibility to change on a dime as things unfold is incredible. He never approaches challenges with a set of canned presentations and always steps out of his comfort zone to allow the situation to unfold and adapts accordingly.

His exceptional knowledge of human behaviour and what it takes to be great as a person and a team has inspired me personally for many years. Don't get me wrong, Nick will hold up the mirror to individuals and teams and get them to face the brutal reality. He is no pushover, but he does it with such genuine care that it allows defensiveness to fade and progress to occur. Some people may be able to make change happen, but Nick is able to create transformations – taking people to levels they had not previously comprehended, by showing them they can make a difference and that the only thing holding them back is themselves.

The Leadership Arrow is a culmination of Nick's life's work and is a must read for anyone who wants to better themselves, become a better leader, better husband, wife, father, mother or friend, or anyone attempting to change the trajectory of their lives. It's filled with wonderful stories, great insights and practical advice to get you to where you want to go. This book will change your life.

Introduction

"Of course, everyone spoke ill of her profession, but basically, it was all a question of selling her time, like everyone else. Doing things she didn't want to do, like everyone else. Putting up with horrible people, like everyone else. Handing over her precious body and her precious soul in the name of a future that never arrived, like everyone else. Saying that she still didn't have enough, like everyone else. Waiting just a bit longer, like everyone else. Waiting so that she could earn just a little bit more, postponing the realisation of her dreams; she was just too busy right now."

Paulo Coelho[1]

What's the answer so many seek to the question:

"How can I lead myself more effectively to experience the meaningful life I desire and achieve all my goals?

or

"How can I lead others more effectively so together we can lift our performance to new levels of sustainable achievement to really feel good about"?

The answer is Leadership. Leadership that builds, creates, changes and transforms.

Leadership that turns the ordinary into the extraordinary; the mundane into the meaningful; the slog into satisfaction.

Leadership that turns resignation into reaching for new possibilities; resistance into ongoing commitment.

Leadership that transforms those who fight into those who follow.

So much has been written about the importance of Leadership – so why is it there's such a shortage around?

Is it because we don't know what leadership is? Certainly not! It's been studied, researched, measured, debated and well documented.

The word Leadership has its origins in a few root words: Ga-leipan (Gothic); ladan (Old English); laudan (Proto-Germanic); leiden (Dutch); and liethea (Old Nors), with the following meanings:

➢ To go first

➢ The Path

➢ To die for

➢ Causing to follow

By definition, leaders are going somewhere, and whether they're leading themselves or others, they're out in front, leading the way.

Leadership is a Journey.

Figure i: The Leadership Arrow

This book will introduce you to the Leadership Arrow. Based on my 30 years of global consulting experience, it's my humble interpretation of the Leadership journey. It takes everything we know about Leadership and suggests a model that's easy to understand and apply as you travel your own Leadership journey.

Whether you're a business leader, partner, teacher, politician or just want to lead yourself more effectively, this book is written for you. Its examples come from my personal life, from the world of business and lessons learned from so many great leaders I've had the privilege of meeting in my life. Although I've had an academic grounding and still study and expose myself to the latest research and dissertations on Leadership, this book is not, nor does it profess to be, an academic document.

It's a story based on both theory and practical experience.

It's a story based on what works.

It's a story of the Leadership journey.

If you'd like to lead yourself more effectively as you strive to achieve your goals, or if you'd like to know how to become a more effective leader of others, then read on. This book is for you.

Whether you're a novice leader just starting out on your life's journey, have your first team to lead, or you're a seasoned executive looking to reflect on or improve your leadership ability, this book is for you.

The first three chapters are about the essence of personal leadership. They will reveal some truths about how we limit ourselves; how effective leaders approach life; and the inevitable challenges leaders face on a daily basis. These chapters will challenge how you're currently leading yourself and suggest a less limiting and more energising approach.

Chapter 4 will introduce you to the concept of the Leadership Arrow as a way of understanding leadership, and the various parts that make up the arrow.

Chapters 5 through 9 will expand on the individual parts of the arrow, using many examples from both personal leadership and organisational leadership.

My intention for this book is not to provide a complete and detailed explanation of the arrow's content. Each part of the arrow is well known and the subject of detailed discussion in many books and academic documents. My intention is, in an easy to understand way, to show the importance of these for effective leadership – to show how they come together in the metaphor of an arrow to create powerful leadership. I've included enough information to satisfy both the experienced reader and those dipping into the subject for the first time. These chapters have numerous practical hints and tips to make the themes and concepts both personal and practical.

Chapters 10 and 11 recognise that we can't achieve success without the support of other people, and looks at some critical interpersonal habits that can and do impact negatively on our leadership effectiveness. Again, there are many practical suggestions for implementation.

Chapter 12 reveals some secrets of leadership communication – the way leaders communicate to make a message stick and to gain commitment.

I've tried to maintain a balance of both personal and business examples in order to make the book interesting to all relevant readers.

If you're only interested in personal leadership please note that chapters 7 and 9 have a largely business focus. Feel free to skim through these chapters but please ensure you read the comments on Personal Strategy towards the end of chapter 7.

PART ONE:

THE LEADERS CHALLENGE

"**For this is what the art of archery means; a profound and far reaching contest between the archer and himself.**"

Eugen Herrigel[2]

Chapter 1

I HAVE FINALLY MET THE ENEMY, AND HE IS ME

"I have finally met the enemy, and he is me"

Unknown

Washington DC. Late afternoon. The almost gale force wind had the rain sleeting down at 45 degrees as my wife and I exited our cab outside the Mayflower Hotel. I was on a high having just delivered an exceptionally well-received strategy presentation at the American Society for Training and Development's Annual International Convention. You could say it was one of those 'in the zone' performances that performers in all spheres of life strive to deliver, but don't always achieve.

My thoughts had been focused and clear, the result of hours of preparation. My emotions provided positive energy, packaging my words and content for maximum credible impact, and the presentation just flowed.

As we entered our hotel room, the telephone rang; it was the hotel manager asking whether it would be convenient for him to come up and check our room. I told him it was fine and remarked to my wife that this was really great service, the hotel manager personally checking our room.

A few minutes later there was a knock on our door and the hotel manager walked in with two other people, whom he immediately introduced as CIA agents. I was really taken aback by their presence but he quickly put my mind at rest explaining that the President of the United States, at the time Bill Clinton, was going to be in the hotel that evening for a Democratic Party meeting and they were busy with security checks. Our room was over the side entrance of the hotel where the President would enter.

After a thorough check of our room they apologised for any inconvenience and left.

That evening it was still raining heavily so we decided not to brave the weather, but rather to have an early dinner in the hotel restaurant. Besides, we'd been told that Edgar J Hoover had lunched there daily so we were happy to soak in the historic atmosphere. After a great meal and a bottle of wine, it being too early to go to bed – and us not particularly wanting to go out in the bad weather, my wife suggested we go to the hotel conference centre and see whether we could spot Bill Clinton.

As we walked into the conference centre's foyer it was obvious something was happening. A large area with conference rooms on both sides was crammed full of two kinds of people. Security personnel, obvious by the large ID tags they wore, similar to those worn by the agents who had checked our room, and the press, with their official accreditation tags.

Outside one of the conference rooms a small sign discretely spelled out the occasion: 'Democratic Party Meeting' and a number of strategically placed agents provided a barrier to entry through the door. For us as visitors, this was exciting.

All the available seating was occupied, so we stood in one corner of the lobby just taking in the scene. A short while later the conference room door opened and an agent indicated to the press they could enter the room.

I commented to my wife that this probably indicated a press briefing, which meant it shouldn't be too long before the President came out. By now there were plenty of empty seats vacated by the press, so we chose a couch strategically positioned right opposite the conference room door. A perfect viewing spot.

After about 20 minutes the doors opened again and people started exiting the conference room. We'd worked out the route the President would probably use to get to the side entrance of the building, which gave us only a brief window of opportunity to see him. We kept our gaze firmly on the door to ensure we achieved our goal – to see the President.

*Earlier on I'd noticed a man enter the lobby and sit on a couch opposite us. Now, maybe we didn't belong in that lobby, but this man **definitely** didn't belong. He could best be described as a tramp. He had long unkempt hair in desperate need of a wash. His dirty jeans and t-shirt had also seen better days.*

At this stage he got up off the couch and started staggering unsteadily across the lobby. I soon realised he was walking straight towards us. All the while people were streaming out of the conference room, whilst we were scanning to ensure we achieved our goal. To see the President.

The 'tramp' staggered right up to us – and it would be an understatement for me to say he got into our space. No, he got right into my face, up close and really objectionable.

He said, "Hey man, what's going on here?" I answered that we thought the President was in the room and asked him politely to move on as he was blocking our view.

He didn't move. Standing firmly in front of me he said, "Do you know the man? It's thanks to him I can't find a job. It's thanks to him my daughter can't go to a good school."

I told him we were visitors from South Africa and all we wanted was to see the President, and asked him again to please move as he was blocking our view.

"I know South Africa," he said. "It's that country with the mountain. You people have got the right idea. Your politicians don't perform, you eliminate them."

By now I was getting really angry. Not only was he minimising any chance we had of seeing the President, I also didn't appreciate his comments, so I suggested to my wife we move to another place in the lobby. As I stood up, so he stepped back. His posture changed from slouched to upright, and he stepped back out of my space. He looked intently at me – and I'll never forget those clear blue eyes as he calmly announced, "My apologies Mr. Christelis, the President has now gone. I was only doing my job. Security" – and he flashed his ID.

He explained we were spotted as unknowns by security when we initially entered the lobby and the hotel identified us as guests, but he was obliged to follow security protocol.

The tramp promoted the interests of national safety and security, in this case the protection of the President, and he certainly did a good job. And he did it in a creative, even devious, way.

We all have a tramp inside of us, promoting our inner security, keeping us in our comfort zones in the same way the President was kept in a security zone – and our inner tramp can also get really creative and devious to achieve this. As we travel this book's journey you'll begin to see some of the many tricks the tramp uses to achieve his objective. The only problem is that to keep us in a safety zone, the tramp dupes us into believing we're limited, and in the process, prevents us from achieving our potential.

Leadership is about achieving that potential.

It is important to note that in the context of this book, the tramp is not meant to be a derogatory term or insensitive to poverty, but rather an analogy for that part of our ego which, in attempting to protect us, prevents us from achieving our potential.

The tramp and I – my journey

Inherently you could say I'm a happy person – someone who has travelled life's journey with a positive attitude. I know we're all born that way but this was intrinsically me. Born with incredible potential and the resources to build whatever life I chose for myself.

I grew up in a normal home. It had its ups and downs – with many ups and few downs. However, right back to my earliest memories, I always remember being a fearful child. I needed to go to bed early so I could get comfort from hearing activity in the house, making me feel safe to fall asleep.

I was fearful of World War II, and although we had no fighting in South Africa, I remember my anxious thoughts every time Harvards flew over our house with their distinctive sound, taking off or landing from nearby Rand Airport. I imagined bombs being dropped on our home and you can understand the fear that created in a young child. That resulted in a dread of travelling by plane that lasted quite a few years.

I suppose those early impressionable years of my life, coinciding with the final years of WW2, has something to do with the fact that I abhor violence in any way.

Playing it safe

My school years went by with no great achievements or problems. I was in a comfort zone with the fearful me always there – but under control. However the reality was that my fearfulness always made me play it safe. And playing it safe resulted in an average life, as playing it safe always does.

Life begins at the end of our comfort zone

Then one day I suddenly became confronted by the reality of my fearfulness; my lack of self-confidence.

I matriculated early at 16 and went off to university to study psychology, and it hit me like a bolt of lightning. I felt comfortable, even confident, in the comfort of home or school, which were pretty controlled and regimented but familiar. University though was a whole different world. One where I had to make it on my own – I had to lead myself.

There was this fearful, if outwardly seemingly confident, child, thrown into an adult world, and I discovered I had the biggest lack of confidence and inferiority complex you could imagine. I was scared to go to university. I would cry silently to myself every single day as I prepared to go off to lectures and confront the challenges that took me out of my comfort zone, out of my safe space and into the unfamiliar.

I was my own worst enemy

"If you get the inside right, the outside will fall into place."

Eckhart Tolle[3]

And then one day, not having the courage to face the challenge of going to lectures and socialising with people I hardly knew, people I imagined as being more capable than me, I decided to stay home. At that moment the leader in me said, "No, this is ridiculous; you're no better or worse than anyone else. Pull yourself together. Get out and just do what you have to do."

It was like a switch had been thrown. I'd taken control simply by changing my thoughts about myself. I was the same person – but it was a different me. The real ME; the ME I was born to be; the ME with potential. The same potential each and every human being has. But to achieve that potential requires taking accountability for yourself and your life. It means you have to lead yourself – and leading yourself is an ongoing, never ending journey you have to go on before you can lead others.

Did I become a confident, socially adept, successful human being overnight? A leader? No, but I started an exciting journey – a journey of discovering the real me. A journey of discovering who I am and what is really important to me. Am I there yet? No! Like all growth, it's an ongoing journey, but the journey itself is leadership development in action.

A journey driven by my potential, not by my fears and doubts

"Nothing will work unless you do."

Maya Angelou[4]

If I'm honest my journey has been an ongoing battle between myself and my tramp. I can honestly say I do win most of the battles, but the tramp is always there, and he has many guises. He's like the big bad wolf in the Little Red Riding Hood story – an imposter, disguised as an older, wiser confidant who makes me feel safe; my protector. Seemingly my friend; someone with my best interests at heart; someone I can trust. Yet behind the friendly façade is an enemy who can and will eventually defeat me by reducing my life to a pittance of my potential, and in the process make me feel comfortable with less than I can achieve.

The tramp comes between me and my potential – between me and my life

We all have a tramp. He's living in our heads. The tramp represents our defence mechanisms, which are a part of our everyday psychological life. Anna Freud[5] defined in detail the defense mechanisms sketched out by her father, Sigmund, in her book, *The Ego and the Mechanisms of Defense.* "They are there to protect us; to keep us safe, but we should remember that they are not just an unconscious protective measure to prevent us from connecting with potentially dangerous instinctual desires and harmful environmental situations."

They also protect us from the anxiety of confronting our own weaknesses and foibles, and in the process prevent us from growing and thriving.

Denial is the most generic defense mechanism used by the tramp, and it underlies so many of the others that are documented in the literature. When you use denial you simply refuse to believe the truth or reality about yourself or an experience. 'No, I'm just a social drinker', is a good example. We use denial to distance ourselves from anything we're uncomfortable with or that threatens us. Whatever the mechanism is, it comes from the instinctual 'flight or fight' response we all have. When threatened or feeling inadequate, we attack (become angry or aggressive) or we withdraw (avoid and become passive).

Try the following self-assessment. Do you:

> get uncomfortable when faced with an uncertain future?

> worry about people realising you're not as clever as they think you are?

> often try to avoid conflict or confrontation?

> use conflict and confrontation in order not to appear weak?

> doubt whether you have what it takes to really succeed and sometimes fear you'll be uncovered as a fraud, so you don't try, or you 'cover your butt'?

> loathe the idea of taking on a goal and failing miserably?

> take on any challenge simply to prove yourself?

> sometimes 'catastrophise' about worst-case scenarios, particularly when you're contemplating making a change or taking a chance on something new?

> find it difficult to trust others or situations?

If you answered yes to any of these questions it's an indication you're human; you have a tramp. However, the more questions you answer yes to, the more your tramp is in control and the less you're leading yourself. Recognising the tramp is the first necessary step to reducing his influence and the beginning of leading yourself.

No-one relishes the prospect of being rejected, criticised, or having their intelligence questioned. No-one savours giving feedback others may find upsetting or having to retrench staff. No-one likes to raise issues that could raise the ire of managers above, much less jeopardise their own job. But unless you're willing to take such risks throughout your life, you'll never be able to achieve the bigger – and yes, more risk-laden – goals that really light you up and align with your purpose and *vision*.

You have to be willing to risk the familiarity and safety of where you are now to create a more rewarding future.

Being in either fight (attack) or flight (avoid) puts you into survival mode, and there's a huge difference between 'surviving' and 'thriving.'

'Surviving' is the realm of the tramp.

'Thriving' is the result of Leadership.

> *"Incredible potential resides in all of us. Most people spend a lot of time suppressing it."*

"When the archer misses the centre of the target, he turns around and seeks the cause of his failure in himself."

Confucius[6]

Chapter 2

LEADERSHIP AND CHOICE

In life there are two possible states. Surviving or thriving. Surviving happens in a comfort zone. Thriving can only happen in a state of growth. The comfort zone might feel safe but the reality is it's not even maintaining the status quo – it's going backwards, because as you stand still, life and others are moving forward, which means you're falling behind. An easy way of conceptualising this is by using the concept *above the line* and *below the line*.

ABOVE THE LINE is a state of growing and thriving.

Words that describe the state of living ABOVE THE LINE:

➤ Controlling own destiny

➤ Living without limits

➤ Learning

➤ Making it happen

➤ Abundance

➤ Confidence

➤ Going for dreams

➤ Challenging

➤ Creating and exploring new things

➤ Embracing change

➤ Being myself

➤ Courage to act

How do you feel reading the above words? What emotions surface? What does it make you feel like doing? How would followers feel and act if they felt like this?

ABOVE THE LINE is driven by our potential.

ABOVE THE LINE is the world of Leadership.

BELOW THE LINE is a state of stagnating while living in a comfort zone.

Words that describe the state of living BELOW THE LINE:

➤ Being controlled

➤ Insecure

➤ Boring life

➤ Just getting by

➤ Procrastinating

➤ Playing it safe

➤ Settling for less

➤ Anger

➤ Resentment

➤ Blaming

➤ Accepting

➤ Entitlement

> Watching it happen
> Feel like an imposter – I'm just lucky
> Forging on

How does reading the above words make you feel? See the difference?

BELOW THE LINE is the tramp at work.

Signs the tramp is at work

> You get motivated about a dream or a goal but pretty quickly the motivation wanes.
> You procrastinate.
> You justify why you cannot or should not do this at this time.
> You avoid your goal by distracting yourself through doing so-called 'urgent' activities.
> You tell yourself you were not meant to achieve that kind of success.
> You label others who achieve as lucky.
> When you do succeed, you call yourself lucky.
> You feel like an imposter.
> You are constantly sceptical.
> You attack when you know you're wrong or when someone disagrees with you.
> You don't like to be challenged.

It's better to be above the line, green, growing and thriving. When you live below the line you might feel comfortable, but the truth is you are slowly decaying.

A perfect illustration of the above

A man was walking down the road when he picked up two unusually shaped acorns. On arriving home he noticed one of the acorns was much more unusual than the other, so he placed it in a glass enclosed ornament cabinet that stood in his lounge. The other acorn he threw out the window.

Twenty years later the man wanted to remove something from the ornament cabinet and in doing so accidently knocked over the acorn that had been sitting there for twenty years. Guess what happened to that acorn? It broke up into dust. Yet right outside his lounge window stood a forty-foot tall oak tree. From the minute the discarded acorn hit the earth all those years ago it was committed by nature to grow. It had no choice. But growth meant pain and suffering, as growth so often can. Storms, wind, drought, disease, humans, animals – and still it grew into a forty foot oak tree. Yet the other acorn, sitting on the shelf of life in a lovely comfort zone, died.

The lesson

There's a fundamental law or principle in science that states very simply that every living thing is either in a state of growth or decay. There's no standing still – this applies to both individuals and teams.

When we set stretch goals for ourselves and bump our heads; when life throws its curve balls and challenges at us and when people do what people will invariably do, we're given the gift of an opportunity to grow or equally the opportunity to decay.

However there are some people reading this who are thinking – 'Well, I'm actually in quite a high powered position. I've achieved many of my goals but I'm worried that one day I'll be found out….'

The imposter syndrome

N.B. In my 27 years of consulting I've found that possibly 4 out of 10 senior executives at some stage feel like imposters. The incidence of the imposter syndrome is slightly higher in women; the incidence is even higher in affirmative action appointees. My experience matches the experiences of many others who have written about the Imposter Syndrome.[7]

If you're one of those people who push or attack your way through your doubts to success, the fact that you disobeyed the tramp can make you feel like an imposter; a fraud. This comes from tramp thoughts such as, "What are you doing here? You're going to get found out." Academy Award winning actress Kate Winslet said: "I'd wake up in the morning before going to a shoot and think, 'I can't do this, I'm a fraud.'"

Most of my clients who have experienced the Imposter Syndrome would never say, "I feel like an imposter" and yet when I bring up the concept, they say, "How did you know?"

I remember a client – an executive in a large consumer business in Cyprus – who complained about a little voice in his head that was constantly criticising almost everything he did. He never felt he deserved his successes, including his current executive position. He even had frequent thoughts that he was stupid.

At some point he mentioned, almost incidentally, that he had a Ph.D. from Harvard.

"You have a Ph.D. from Harvard?" I exclaimed. "How could you possibly get a Ph.D. from Harvard if you're stupid?"

His answer convinced me I was dealing with his tramp: "I was lucky."

Nobel Laureate Maya Angelou once said, "I've written 12 books now but each time I think 'Uh oh, they're going to find out. I've run a game on everybody, and they're going to find me out.'"

Attitudes, beliefs, actions or reactions, direct or indirect messages we received from our parents or other significant people in our lives as we grew up formed the DNA of the tramp.

This tramp will keep us safe by preventing us from leaving our comfort zone, or from seeing and accepting critical feedback. The tramp is what gets us into denial and prevents us from dealing with reality. In the process it will prevent us from easily accepting success when we achieve it. At a deep level we don't feel we deserve it and negative behaviour such as anger, withdrawal or blame serves the purpose of covering up feelings of inadequacy.

I remember well at the end of my matric year, the headmaster came into our class and asked each one of us to stand up and say what we intended doing after we matriculated. I told him I wanted to go to university to study psychology. His comment, "Christelis, you should change your ambitions. I don't think you'll ever see the inside of a university." Sure, I was never a star student, always passing with comfortable grades, but that really hit me hard.

That year, out of 66 matrics only 22 passed and I was one of the lucky ones, and that's how I felt – lucky. Another victory for the tramp.

The tramp's impact on business

Most businesses fail, not because of the external environment, the competition or forces in the marketplace. Most businesses are brought down from within through an inability to stretch, change and adapt as the world unfolds. Why? Because of arrogance, incorrect priorities and an inability to learn and change; a lack of leadership.

This is the internal battle between the organisation's potential of growing value and its very own tramp; its own denial mechanism. Yet we must remember that organisations don't make profits, *people do*. Organisations don't succeed or fail, *their people do*. And these people all bring their own personal tramps to work with them, keeping them safe, secure and comfortable, and in the process, preventing them from reaching their full potential.

Organisational culture will drive behaviour and determine whether people will work above or below the line – whether they will be empowered or not.

Table 2.1: Comparison

ABOVE THE LINE companies		BELOW THE LINE companies
1. Personal success stems from *taking* risk	VS	1. Personal success stems from *avoiding* risk
2. Expectations exceed results	VS	2. Results exceed expectations
3. From *why* and *what* to do	VS	3. To *how* to do and *who* did it
4. Everything is permitted, unless expressly forbidden	VS	4. Everything is forbidden, unless expressly permitted
5. Problems are seen as opportunities	VS	5. Opportunities are seen as problems
6. People accept personal accountability	VS	6. People play the blame game
Ichak Adizes[8]		

Jim Collins, in his book *How the Mighty Fall,* describes organisational denial as follows: "Leaders discount negative data, amplify positive data and put a positive spin on ambiguous data. Those in power start to blame external factors for setbacks rather than accept responsibility."[9]

It's in the culture: The monkeys' experiment

A great experiment illustrates how getting into denial and playing it safe creates a below the line culture and restricts behaviour. Twelve monkeys were placed in a cage with a rope hanging from the ceiling. Each day the researchers placed bananas at the top of the rope. The monkeys soon learned how to climb the rope to get a banana. This very quickly became an easily learned 'success' habit.

At this stage any monkey who started climbing the rope was hit with a stream of water from a power hose creating an uncomfortable experience that prevented the monkeys from continuing their climb to the bananas.

This hosing happened each time any monkey attempted to climb the rope. Soon all monkeys learned not to climb the rope. At this point the researchers removed one monkey from the cage and replaced it with a new monkey. Very quickly, seeing the bananas at the top of the rope, the new monkey began its climb only to be stopped by the remaining 11 monkeys. After a few days of this being repeated the new monkey no longer attempted to climb the rope. It had learned the lesson (as new recruits in a business quickly learn what is acceptable and unacceptable behaviour).

The researchers now removed a second monkey, also replacing it with a new one. The new monkey followed the same procedure, saw the bananas, jumped onto the rope and was quickly pulled down by the remaining monkeys. This procedure was followed until all original 12 monkeys who had experienced the high pressure hose were removed from the cage. Not only did the new monkeys, who had never experienced the high pressure hose, not attempt to climb the rope, they even prevented rope climbing by any further new monkeys that entered the cage. Not climbing the rope was now in the culture. It's the way we do things around here.

Exercise

1. Recall an instance when you had the opportunity to improve your life or make a difference at work; an opportunity to be part of a cutting-edge team; the chance to take on a stretch assignment. A situation in which your decision could have changed the work dynamic in your group for the better; a decision that could have improved or even positively changed your life. But in this instance, you didn't capitalise on the opportunity or decision in front of you. You dipped below the line. With hindsight, you know what you should have done, but didn't do it.

2. On a sheet of paper, list all the thoughts and feelings that prevented you from taking this action. For instance, one thought might be, "My analyst told me it was smarter to do nothing rather than expose myself to criticism." Or "I was afraid of looking bad in front of my boss." Or, "This is not the time to do it."

3. On that same piece of paper, list all the potential positive outcomes that might have been produced by taking the action you refused to take. What learning might you have gained? What skills might have you acquired? How might it have made you a better manager and leader?

This exercise isn't for the faint of heart. Just as many of us still regret not asking that one girl to dance, many of us are sorry we didn't ask for that transfer, take on the tough assignment, or make that life or business transforming decision. But recognising this regret is crucial. Breaking free from the immobilising denial power of the tramp starts with learning how to notice when your tramp is at work. Only when you're aware of being BELOW THE LINE are you in a position to do something different – to find an antidote for the tramp.

Only then can you start the real journey of Leadership. We'll deal with this in more detail in the next chapter.

Nobody lives above or below the line exclusively, however make it a habit to ask these key questions as you face the challenges of daily living.

"At this moment, am I being ABOVE THE LINE or am I being BELOW THE LINE?"

"Am I leading myself or am I being led by the tramp?"

"Destiny is no matter of chance. It is a matter of choice. It is not a thing to be waited for; it is a thing to be achieved."

Williams Jennings Bryan[10]

Chapter 3

LEADING FROM ABOVE THE LINE

"I don't fix problems, I fix my thinking. Then problems fix themselves."

Louise Hay[11]

Personal story

It's a warm October evening in 2002. Thirty families are gathered in a park in Woodmead, Johannesburg, for a braai and a personal development experience.

My colleague Dr Deon van Zyl and I have designed the process and are the facilitators for the evening.

The personal growth opportunity is going to come from three guests who have been invited to the event. These guests each have a story to tell. The idea is that after they tell their stories, the families would have the opportunity to enter into discussion with them and hopefully some great life lessons would be learned.

The first guest to tell his story is a dynamic and highly successful Irishman with an incredible sense of humour – Billy Gallagher, Food and Beverage Director of Southern Sun Hotels. He begins his story and tells how he was shot in an attempted car hijacking, the bullet severing his spinal cord. He spent nine months in hospital, a total quadriplegic, able to move nothing but his neck. He describes the roller coaster of emotions all human beings would go through under such circumstances. He tells the other families, "I went from being a peacock to a feather."

*After nine months of emotional turmoil '**he came back.**' Still a quadriplegic, he successfully resumed work as Food and Beverage Director for Southern Sun Hotels with a full time nurse to attend to his physical needs and a personal assistant to do the physical work. **All he had was his brain and his experience – it was all he needed.** His highly successful career back on track, he was subsequently appointed as the honorary Life President of the World Association of Chefs; a great accolade for a great man. He has also since then held the positions of Chairman of the School of Tourism and Hospitality Studies (2006), Executive Director for the Centre of Culinary Excellence, (2005), and Director of Communication and PR for the Southern Sun Hotel Group (2004).*

*The second guest to tell his story was Geoff Hilton-Barber. Geoff was studying actuarial science at university when he got retinosa pigmentosa (a degenerative eye disease). Within two weeks he became totally blind. He also described to the families the roller coaster of emotions he experienced, from anger to resentment to depression – to intense feelings of hopelessness and absolute despair. He refused to believe any worthwhile future lay ahead for him. But as he described it, one day something happened and **he lifted himself out of the depths of despair and put himself back on the road to a positive and desirable future.***

Today, besides running a successful business, he has become the first blind sailor to sail an ocean single-handedly, successfully navigating the treacherous Indian Ocean from Durban, South Africa to Freemantle, Australia, defying friends, family and experts who termed his endeavour a "suicide mission." And he's climbed Mount Kilimanjaro. This is far more than most sighted people will ever do!

The third guest, probably after Nelson Mandela the most incredible human being I have ever had the privilege of meeting, was Zak Yacoob. Born in KwaZulu

Natal in 1948, he contracted meningitis at a young age leaving him totally blind. Despite this he embarked on a journey to follow his purpose. He studied law, becoming an advocate and then a judge. His journey culminating where he finds himself today – as a judge who helped write South Africa's Constitution and who has served as one of the justices of the Constitutional Court as well as serving as the Deputy Chief Justice of South Africa.

After the guests told their stories the invited families asked questions.

➤ *How did these people overcome their hurdles and challenges?*
➤ *How did they lift themselves out of the depths of despair and hopelessness and become role models for what every one of us can achieve, irrespective of circumstances?*
➤ *How did they lead themselves to a better future?*

At the end of the evening, three very clear and powerful lessons emerged. The first two relate to this chapter. The third lesson forms the topic of a later chapter.

Lesson one: Don't hang on to hurdles and obstacles you can't change

If you do you'll be rooted to the spot and go nowhere. This relates to the Alcoholics Anonymous credo: 'God grant me the strength to change the things that I can, to accept the things that I can't, and the wisdom to know the difference between the two.'

As Geoff pointed out: "If you want to know what you're doing to yourself by hanging on to things you can do nothing about, put some superglue on the floor and stand on it. You can't move forward and this is what happens to so many of us. We become stuck where we are because we keep hanging on to circumstances we can do nothing about."

Lesson two: "If it's going to be, it's up to me"

All three guests said they could remember the day their breakthrough happened; the day the penny dropped. The day they moved from below the line to above the line. As one of them said, "You wake up one morning and you realise, if it's going to be – it's up to me."

It's the moment we take responsibility for creating the lives we desire.

It's the moment we understand and accept the toughest accountability there is.

For me that moment was the morning I woke too fearful to go to university. It was the day I accepted, "If it's going to be – it's up to me." It's the day I took responsibility for my own life.

As Viktor Frankl (an Austrian neurologist and psychiatrist as well as a Holocaust survivor) so eloquently put it, "Between a stimulus and our response lies the greatest privilege we have as human beings. The privilege of choice."[12]

As life happens, we don't have to respond habitually or in an automatic way. We can *choose* our response, accepting that our choices ultimately create our lives.

And why is this so tough to accept? Because if we accept the privilege of choice it means when we look in the mirror, today or at any time in the future, what we see reflected there, what we have achieved, has nothing at all to do with our circumstances, the economy, politics, management, our partner or our childhood. It's totally the result of the choices we made when those things happened.

The state of our lives is the result of the choices we make as life unfolds, so we must choose wisely. No matter what our circumstances are or what's happening in our lives, we can choose how we're going to respond. This puts us in the driver's seat. This puts us in control.

Above or below the line?

When things don't go according to plan, when life throws us a curve ball, when others' behaviour frustrates our intentions, we reach a choice point.

It's when things go wrong that successful people have created the edge by choosing to go 'Above the Line', and failures will lose the edge by choosing to go 'Below the Line.'

Below the Line lies excuse making, blaming others, confusion and an attitude of helplessness, while Above the Line we find a sense of reality, ownership, commitment, solutions to problems and determined action.

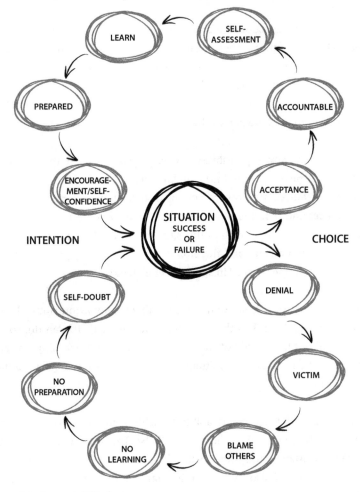

Figure 3.1: Accountability loop

Below the line is the Victim Loop. Above the line is the Accountability Loop.

Our **intention** refers broadly to whatever it is we want to achieve at any point in time. It could refer to our long-term vision or a short-term goal or objective we want to achieve, or simply to any set of circumstances we want to create for ourselves.

The **situation** we currently find ourselves in will be either **positive** in relation to our intention, meaning we are making meaningful progress, or it will be **negative,** meaning our intention is being frustrated in some way.

At this point we can choose whether we're going to move into either an **Accountability Loop** or a **Victim Loop.** This is a choice point where we're free to exercise our privilege of choice. No one forces us to make a particular choice; we do it of our own free will.

The Victim Loop is characterised by:

Denial that I have any responsibility or have played any role in the situation I find myself in (the tramp in action). This kind of thinking implies I'm a **Victim** of my circumstances or of others' actions or behaviour. I start **Blaming** my circumstances and pointing fingers at others or my circumstances. They are to blame for me finding myself in this situation. Something or someone out there causes my problems and therefore the solution to my problems is out there, in the situation itself or in someone else's hands.

It's not for me to do anything. Something out there or somebody must change or do something. There's nothing I should change or that I can do, so **No Learning** takes place inside of me, and because I'm not learning I'm **Not Preparing** myself to handle this situation going forward, leaving me in a state of **Self-Doubt.**

I start losing confidence in my ability to achieve my intention. I go back into the situation and repeat the cycle with **No Learning** and **Self-Doubt,** more **Denial, Blame,** and more feeling like I'm a **Victim,** which becomes a downward spiral. I also call it a **Maintenance Loop** because it maintains itself.

The **Victim Loop** results in feelings of anger, frustration and helplessness, raising stress levels but also leading to a state of resignation; accepting a sub-par life. So many people live as victims. So sad. So unnecessary. The **Victim Loop** is living BELOW THE LINE.

One of my clients suggested that it's more than a maintenance loop: he called it a **Doom Loop.**

There is always another choice: **The Accountability Loop.**

The Accountability Loop is characterised by:

Acceptance that as long I'm in the situation, I'm **Accountable** for my contribution – for the way I respond or don't respond to the situation. I then do a **Self-Assessment**, asking myself questions like:

➤ What is this testing in me?

➤ What do I need to learn in order to handle this more constructively and positively?

➤ What am I doing that's making the situation worse for me? What should I stop doing?

➤ What am I not doing that's just aggravating the situation?

➤ What can I do to make it better?

➤ What options are open to me right now that will move this situation forward?

➤ What's the next positive step I can take towards my intentions?

These **Accountability** questions put the ball firmly in my court, kick-starting the **Leader** in me and putting me on a **Learning** path, making me better **Prepared** to face this and future similar situations. **Encouraging** me to move forward, while building my **Self-Confidence.**

This is called a **Growth Loop.** I am learning and growing as life throws its challenges at me, as it always does. This is living ABOVE THE LINE.

Look at the sketch and replace the word 'Intention' with the words 'My Life.' Follow both loops to get an insight into yourself. Ponder on your thoughts and feelings for a moment. What do you realise?

Choosing to survive

Viktor Frankl was a Jewish psychiatrist who spent three years during World War 2 living in unspeakable circumstances in several of the most notorious Nazi concentration camps.

While imprisoned, Frankl realised he had one single freedom left: he had the power to determine his response to the horror unfolding around him.

And so he chose to imagine.

He imagined his wife and the prospect of seeing her again. He imagined himself teaching students after the war about the lessons he'd learned.

Frankl survived and went on to chronicle his experiences and the wisdom he had learned from them.

"A human being is a deciding being", he wrote in his 1946 book, *Man's Search for Meaning,* which sold more than 10 million copies. "Between stimulus and response there is a space. In that space is our power to choose our response. In our response lies our growth and our freedom."

Frankl's description of how he survived is a classic example of a **Growth Loop**. He started by **Accepting** the reality of his situation, and then accepted **Accountability** for himself and his reaction to his circumstances. He accepted he could choose his reaction and so he did a **Self–Assessment**: What was this testing in him? What could he do to handle the situation in the best possible way? How were others coping? In his search for a solution he realised how other prisoners would very quickly deteriorate and die after they lost hope, so he **Learned** to actively manage his thinking by forcing himself to imagine his life after his ordeal was over. Because of this he felt **Prepared** to handle his daily challenges with **Encouragement** and **Self-Confidence.**

The young women's activist and Nobel Laureate, Malala Yousafzai, chose to defy the Taliban and demanded that girls be allowed to receive an education. She was shot in the head by a Taliban gunman but survived. Her constant challenging of a system that she saw as oppressive and her comment subsequent to her being shot – "They can only shoot your body; they cannot shoot your dreams" – is a remarkable example of choosing to live above the line, accepting accountability and continually looking for solutions rather than going below the line and playing the blame game. The relationship between living above the line and being seen as a leader should be clear. Leadership begins with self-leadership, and self-leadership can only exist above the line.

Think of great leaders you know. Think of the times you have exhibited leadership. Look at the graphic above. Were they or you above or below the line? Ask yourself, "Who would I follow?" Someone who's above the line or someone who's below the line?

Victim cycle self-assessment

➤ Has negative feedback from someone surprised you just when you thought you were doing fine?

➤ Have you ever blamed others and pointed fingers when things have gone wrong?

➤ Have you ever kept a paper trail or covered your butt in case things went wrong?

➤ Have you ever thought, "I'm not going attend to it…. it's not my job?"

➤ Have you ever felt you had no control over circumstances?

➤ Have you ever just waited to see if a situation would simply go away or resolve itself?

➤ Do you ever not take initiative because you don't 'own the business'?

➤ Do you ever complain about being taken advantage of?

➤ Do you ever feel you are treated unfairly?

If you answered 'yes' to any of these questions it's an indication you're 'only human' and that you make the occasional visit **Below the Line**. However, the more 'yes' answers you have the more likely it is you may be stuck **Below the Line** in the **Victim Loop** on a given issue or circumstance, or even in the broader context of your life.

All the choices we make in life can be characterised as **ABOVE THE LINE** or **BELOW THE LINE**. There will be numerous mentions of this throughout the remaining chapters.

Recognising that you are **Below the Line** and in the 'Victim Loop' is the starting point for getting better results and helping you relieve some of the stress that comes from feeling stuck. Where does playing the victim game get you? Answer: Nowhere, and fast!

When you allow your tramp to give you permission to do nothing about your situation, when you don't accept accountability, don't acknowledge your responsibility, don't admit having done wrong, don't face the facts, don't give up the sympathy that a victim's story attracts, and don't look for what else you can do to achieve results or improve your life – your behaviour gets you nowhere. And when you're going nowhere there can be, by definition, no leadership.

As I've said, it's normal for humans to dip below the line, as long as you don't stay there too long, because playing the victim role only dulls your senses and discourages your imagination from discovering creative solutions. Remember, getting above the line is a process, not a singular event, and the road to results is strewn with hindrances and obstacles that can easily push even the most accountable person back below the line – particularly if he/ she stops asking the central question, "What else can I do to rise above my circumstances and achieve the results I want?"

A long time ago and far away, in a village there was a wise old man. He was so wise the villagers always went to him if they had a problem. In this village also, was a young man who thought he was as wise, if not wiser than the old man, but no villager would ever go to him with a problem so he regularly put the old man to the test, in public, trying to show him up, but could never succeed.

One day, the village marketplace was full of people doing their shopping, when into the marketplace walked the young man with his hands behind his back. Everyone knew that another challenge was imminent. At the top of his voice, the young man said, "Old man. I have a bird in my hands behind my back. If you are as wise as these people think, then tell me; is the bird dead or alive?" Without hesitation the old man said, "Young man, if I tell you the bird is dead you will bring it out from behind your back and let it fly away, proving me wrong. If I tell you the bird is alive, you squeeze it to death, and again, you will prove me wrong."

*He smiled, shook his head and said, "Young man, I don't know why you even asked the question, because **the answer lies in your own hands**."*

When we set stretch goals for ourselves and bump our heads, when life throws its curve balls and challenges at us, when people do what people will invariably do, when the competition act in unexpected ways, we are given the gift of an opportunity to lead and grow, or equally the opportunity to decay.

The answer lies in your own hands.

Exercise

1. Being accountable depends on seeing the bigger picture/all sides of a story. You should therefore begin your assessment by identifying a current situation in which you feel victimised, taken advantage of, or otherwise find yourself dipping Below the Line into the Victim Loop, blaming others or circumstances or even seemingly good reasons for your unhappiness. Once you have selected your story, list the facts of your story in a way that will persuade someone else the situation you find yourself in is not your fault; you really are a victim.

2. Most people quite naturally focus on the facts that make them feel victimised or taken advantage of, while screening out the accountable facts that support their own role in creating or aggravating their circumstances. For this reason, you want to move beyond such filtering, focusing on the accountable facts of your story: that is, the other version of your story where you *describe your own actions or inactions,* which are *contributing to* or *aggravating* your circumstances.

3. Ask yourself:

➤ What can I do to improve this situation?
➤ What is it testing in me?
➤ What do I need to change in my approach?
➤ What else can I do to rise above my circumstances and achieve the results I want?
➤ What can I do more of?
➤ What can I do less of?

ABOVE THE LINE is where leaders live.

BELOW THE LINE is the world of the tramp.

The very definition of Leadership suggests going somewhere. Leadership does not imply standing still. Whether you are leading yourself, a team, or an organisation, the implication is that there's movement in a particular direction.

Chapter 4

THE LEADERSHIP ARROW

Recently I presented a workshop at The International Crime Stoppers Conference, held in Cape Town. Yusuf Abramjee, president of Crime Stoppers in South Africa and vice president of Crime Stoppers International, had managed to bring the conference to Africa for the first time. While interacting with the highest levels within our security system and with leaders in Crime Stoppers worldwide, a few things became blatantly clear.

Globally, crime is escalating rapidly, and as the conference progressed I became more and more aware of just how advanced the police's crime fighting strategy is, the extent to which technology is being utilised in the fight against crime, and the incredible commitment, competence and passion many senior officials have. It also became glaringly obvious that something was lacking, because the results were not what they should or could be. The problem is seemingly two-fold:

> The lack of strategy execution by the majority of police on the ground.

> The lack of collaborative partnerships between all stakeholders in the fight against crime. This includes:

  > The various departments within the security and justice clusters.

  > Partnerships between all other stakeholders who are interested in fighting crime. Politicians, police, the justice system, communities, business and the media. Each is independently doing their best in the quest for a safer world, yet none can do it alone.

To achieve a safer world will depend on bringing these stakeholders together as partners, working together interdependently and collaboratively towards a common purpose, rather than each focusing on their individual contributions; all working above the line trying to find solutions rather than below the line, pointing fingers and slinging arrows at each other. Blame being the name of the game:

> Communities blaming the police for incompetence.

> Police blaming communities for not contributing.

> Police and communities blaming the prosecutorial system for not locking criminals up.

> Prosecutors blaming police for inadequate evidence management.

> The public for not coming forward as witnesses.

> Media that fuel the fire.

> High incidence of corruption.

To bring all these stakeholders together requires Leadership. It cannot be managed or achieved by decree. It must be led.

The very definition of Leadership suggests going somewhere. Leadership does not imply standing still. The essence of Leadership is reflected in the word "followership." Whether you are leading yourself, a team, or an organisation, the implication is that there's movement in a particular direction.

Life implies growth and growth always involves change. Change is what is needed to improve one's situation, to achieve visions and goals, because as the saying goes, "If you do what you've always done, you'll get what you always got." Change means moving from one place to another. Movement. And change and movement require leadership.

Leadership in times of change and crisis

Leadership, of self or others, is needed in times of crisis or in times of change, which can be brought on by:

> Change desired because of dissatisfaction with something in your life such as a career change, leaving a relationship, wanting to start your own business, desiring a better future for yourself, or simply wanting to lose weight.

> Change initiated by others as when management restructures a business or when mergers happen. When a child decides to leave home or when your partner gets retrenched. It can even happen in times when we're comfortable, but a leader comes along who challenges and inspires us to change our comfortable status quo and move in a new direction in all our best interests.

> Change triggered off by dissatisfaction with an environment, such as employees in an organisation striking against poor working conditions or poor pay, as happened at Marikana. Or people rising up for a better life as in the Arab Spring or people objecting to toll roads in South Africa or to austerity measures in Greece.

Leadership in times of imposter contentment

Sometimes, however, it's the leader who arrives at a time of resignation with a less than perfect life or an unhappy situation and who incites discontent where previously contentment existed.

People living below the line, accepting their status in life, and perhaps finding some semblance of happiness in a few compensatory corners of their lives. I call this 'imposter happiness.' Making the most of what they have. Yes it's admirable, but it's below the line survival. One day there's a rude awakening and the question gets asked, "Why the hell am I doing this? Is this what life is all about?"

> This state of imposter happiness can be found at every economic or status level in life; it's not restricted to the economically disadvantaged. Note the high levels of 'closet' unhappiness amongst even wealthy or highly successful high profile individuals in the world. Yes, while many are surviving in poverty, there are many surviving in luxury. But surviving isn't thriving. Surviving is a day-to-day state of unhappiness; constantly searching for a way to get through the today. For some without money or education the search is for food, and for others the search is for the next fix that money can buy.

> Imposter happiness is the reason why I have a problem with the so-called 'gratitude' approach to happiness – the theory that being grateful for what you have in your life is the way to happiness. Let me say before I go further that I do agree with the theory, but there's a difference between leadership gratitude and tramp gratitude. If you're grateful for what you have without a leader's vision of where you're going, then what you have is not genuine but imposter happiness. Being grateful leads to imposter happiness when it leads to resignation of unacceptable circumstances in your life. 'Better the devil you know than the devil you don't know' is fertile ground for the tramp. If there's a devil in your life or if you're living in hell, then being grateful will only motivate resignation. This is imposter happiness.

> My experience shows that once you get to a country equivalent of USD70 000 per annum, any increase in earnings results in a miniscule increase in happiness.

And so we make the most of our lives until one day we wake up in a state of dissatisfaction; we have reached a choice point. We could go below the line, play the victim role, feel sorry for ourselves and get into the doom loop, or we could get above the line and lead ourselves and others towards a better future.

Leadership and loss

Leadership has the potential to emerge anytime there is dissatisfaction with the status quo and anytime change is initiated by you, others or the system, because change always brings with it a sense of loss of:

➤ comfort and security

➤ direction

➤ coping with the situation

➤ control

➤ relationships

All the above examples bring us to choice points. We can either move below the line, listen to the tramp, get into denial, be a victim, blame others and wallow in self-pity, or move above the line, leading ourselves and others to a new improved tomorrow.

Enter the tramp

He will tell us to accept our situation; to be grateful; that we're lucky to have what we've got; that we don't deserve or have the capability to have more in life. So we get into denial, putting our head down, taking it day by day, with all the symptoms of unhappiness which we blame on others and our circumstances. We eat more than we should; drink more; become irritable, demotivated and defensive. We're surviving but certainly not thriving. But the day we wake up and recognise our 'imposter happiness' – that we've been living below the line in a fool's paradise – that's the day serious unhappiness, dissatisfaction and even depression could knock on our door.

Enter the Leader

Leaders spell out reality and then give hope.

"Only when darkness recognises the absence of light will the call for light appear."

St Augustine of Hippo[13]

A leader will hold up the mirror for self and others. The leader will take a selfie and encourage us to take a selfie of ourselves and our lives. A leader is prepared to confront the sometimes brutal truths the tramp wants us to deny. The emptiness of our lives; the sad state of our relationships; the potential of our business that's not being tapped; the state of our nation.

A leader will paint a vision of what's possible; a vision of a better tomorrow, of a future that inspires and enables people and themselves to act.

A leader will take us above the line, encouraging us to be accountable and do whatever needs to be done to achieve our vision. They make us feel that despite the reality of our current situation, there's always hope for a better future and that future lies in our own hands.

Leaders spell out reality and give hope.

Marikana: A leaderless tragedy?

Did the Marikana[14] tragedy in South Africa happen because of a lack of leadership? I think so. No overall leadership emerged from the miners, unions, police or the government. The energy of dissatisfaction can, as we have seen, become destructive, as happened with the deaths of so many human beings at Marikana – an unforgivable tragedy. Where was the leadership to give hope; to inspire a shared vision of a win/win future; to suggest a future all stakeholders could buy into? Sure, there were negotiators, people whose job it was to protect the interests of the independent stakeholders, but no true visible leadership emerged. Leadership that united all parties around a common win/win purpose. It's highly possible the various negotiators espoused the words win/win, but were they believable? Leadership is not what you say, it's who you are.

Did the dissatisfaction happen overnight? No, it never does. It simmers and can stay like that indefinitely or until a trigger point causes it to surface and disrupt our imposter happiness.

At this point, if we stay below the line it has the potential of becoming destructive, with arrows being slung at those whom we blame for our situation (even bullets as at Marikana), putting us firmly into a doom loop. Or we can move above the line, pointing our arrows in the direction of a vision of a better future by taking accountability for our actions and searching for what we can do to create that better future for ourselves.

This was the kind of leadership we saw from Nelson Mandela. As the old apartheid era gasped its last breaths and naysayers predicted doom for our country, as the AWB drove its trucks through the doors of the World Trade Centre where our future was being negotiated, so did Madiba point our arrow towards a new future – a future of a better "South Africa for all people, irrespective of colour." A win/win vision. This kind of leadership is often written about and many brilliant people have unpacked the qualities, characteristics and behaviours of these leaders, trying to make leadership a tangible, easily doable thing.

Leadership is personal

Let me reiterate one thing. Leadership is not about what you do – it's about who you are, so leadership starts off with me personally. My self-leadership defines why I'm here, who I am and where I'm going. It's my philosophy about life and living. It's my personal journey. This is the 'me' people will follow when I suggest a common journey to travel on. This is what gives a leader that vital ingredient called credibility, without which leadership is not possible. So as you read on please remember that leading yourself is the starting point. It's the genesis of leadership.

We cannot lead anyone else if we can't lead ourselves. As we go through the rest of this book any reference I make to Leadership applies both to personal Leadership as well as that of others. I urge you to consider how what you're reading applies to you and your life before considering how it applies to leading others. The examples I give will relate to both personal and interpersonal or organisational Leadership. One of the most respected Leadership schools in the USA, The Centre for Creative Leadership, spells it out convincingly: 'Leadership development is personal development.'

My intention here is to take you on a journey beginning with **personal Leadership,** moving through **interpersonal Leadership** to **team** or **organisational Leadership.**

Figure 4.1: The Leadership Arrow

I have for some time been using the concept of The Leadership Arrow to develop Leadership in my client companies and have been thrilled at the feedback I've received, even from really seasoned and sometimes sceptical CEOs.

An arrow today is like a golf club, a scientifically designed implement. It largely consists of three parts, all playing a vital role in hitting its target.

1. *The Arrowhead*. This is the primary *functional* part of the arrow and plays the largest part in determining the arrow's *purpose*. It gives direction and impact. It contains the *intention* of the arrow.

2. *The Shaft*. This is the primary *structural* element of the arrow, on which the other parts of the arrow are attached. It gives form, momentum and energy.

3. *Fletchings*, sometimes called vanes, are found at the back of the arrow and act as airfoils. They are designed to keep the arrow pointed in the

direction of travel by strongly damping down any tendency for the shaft to pitch or yaw. Without fletchings an arrow could still have incredible energy and travel far, but it would easily be deflected off target by environmental forces.

It's important to note that these three parts of an arrow are interdependent. All three must operate to standard and be aligned with one another for the arrow to fly to its full potential.

The arrow is a great analogy for life or for business.

The Arrowhead

The Arrowhead represents intention. It defines purpose and meaning. It answers the following questions:

> Why am I here?
> Why does this organisation or business exist?
> Where am I going?
> How can we ensure success?

The answers to these questions are all long-term considerations. They can be revisited regularly, but invariably the answers remain fundamentally the same.

The Arrowhead creates the potential for **Leadership**. No Arrowhead, no Leadership.

The Arrowhead provides purpose and meaning to all we do from moment to moment. It's where passion is created, and it's this intense passion that drives:

> deep commitment
> ground breaking innovation
> phenomenal perseverance
> incredible resilience

Without passion, none of these things are possible:

➤ It's our highest Intention

➤ It's the fire that fuels the furnace of our souls

➤ It's our *raison d'être*, our 'Reason for existence'

➤ It gives life to what we do

➤ It makes 'the daily grind' truly worthwhile

The Shaft

The Shaft is where execution happens. It provides form or structure. It's the shorter-term milestones or goals and plans that we set, that give us the momentum we need to drive the behaviour required to get us to our destination.

The Shaft is the realm of **'managing'**, coming from the root word *manus* meaning hands.

The Fletchings

The constantly changing environment, requests from others, the pressure of required short-term results or just getting through a day, can so easily take us off course as we travel this journey to our destination, and we could land up where we didn't intend to. As Stephen Covey has said, *"Are we so busy climbing the ladder of success that we don't stop to check that it's leaning on the right wall?"*[15]

Fletchings keep us on track as we travel our journey to success, ensuring we always behave within boundaries that are important for us. They dampen the desire to go off course in the interests of expediency or short-term gratification.

The Fletchings help us:

➤ to journey in an incredibly complex moment-to-moment world...

➤ delivering against the short-term expectations on demand...

➤ *in a sustainable way...*

➤ *that we can feel good about.*

The weakest link

The most vulnerable part of an arrow is where the Arrowhead and the Shaft join. This is where the arrow can easily break.

What would happen if you shot the Arrowhead without a Shaft? It would fly a short way and then fall to the ground. Pretty much the same as the many good intentions, dreams and visions people have. Short lived excitement, and then.... nothing.

What would happen if you shot a Shaft without an Arrowhead from a bow? It would accelerate swiftly and probably maintain its momentum for a fair amount of time, but would quickly lose direction and certainly miss the ultimate target. Pretty much like people driven by short-term objectives – achieving them but getting nowhere meaningful or sustainable in the process. Like being on a treadmill. You're running hard, pushing yourself to your limits, achieving the time and distance you've set for yourself, feeling a sense of achievement, but in the process – going nowhere.

The FOC rating

The FOC rating, meaning 'Forward of Centre' score, refers to the position of balance of the arrow. In a good arrow the position of balance is 'Forward of Centre', meaning that it's nearer to the Arrowhead than to the back of the arrow. In any great arrow 60% of the weight is in the Arrowhead and 40% of the weight is in the Shaft.

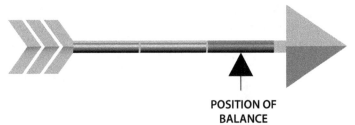

POSITION OF
BALANCE

Figure 4.2: Position of balance

The Leadership challenge

It's this ability – to continuously connect the Arrowhead's purpose and meaning to the short-term objectives and daily grind demanded in the Shaft, in a way that keeps us on track and ensures the sustainability of our success, that ultimately defines leadership.

The leader ensures the mind-set of all stakeholders is 60% on the Arrowhead and 40% on the Shaft.

The Arrowhead should always be in the foreground of our awareness and the Shaft in the background – not vice versa as is the case with most people and in most organisations.

Leaders take us on a meaningful journey to a desirable destination. If not, ask yourself the question, *"Why the hell should I follow?"*

In the next few chapters we will build the arrow.

PART TWO:

INTENTION

Purpose: "The reason why something is done or created or for which something exists."

Oxford Dictionary[16]

Chapter 5

WHY – THE POWER OF PURPOSE

"The least of things with a meaning is worth more in life than the greatest of things without it."

Carl Jung[17]

"The need for purpose is one of the defining characteristics of human beings. Human beings crave purpose and suffer serious psychological difficulties when we don't have it. Purpose is a fundamental component of a fulfilling life."

Steve Taylor[18]

Most individuals or organisations don't make progress because they don't know the single most important discovery for making progress – purpose, and how to use its power to energise and excite themselves or their workforce. As you read this and the next few chapters you'll realise that the purpose and meaning of the Arrowhead begins with the individual, and then, with effective Leadership, spreads through the organisation.

The power of purpose is similar to the energy of light focused through a magnifying glass. Diffused light has little use, but when energy is concentrated – as through a magnifying glass – that same light can set fire to paper. Focus its energy even more, as with a laser beam, and it has the power to cut through steel. Likewise, a clear sense of purpose enables you to focus your efforts on what matters most, compelling you to take risks and push forward, regardless of the odds or obstacles.

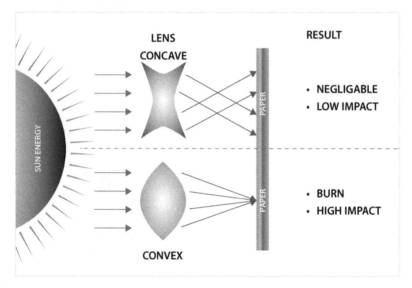

Figure 5.1: The Power of Focus

The cost of losing Purpose

During 2013, newspapers in the UK featured stories of a famous ex-professional soccer player, Paul Gascoigne, who had been struggling with alcoholism. Gazza, as he was known, was the most famous sportsman of his generation, earning 57 caps during his England career and described by the National Football Museum as «the most naturally gifted English midfielder of his generation. After retiring in the early 2000s however, he was in and out of rehab, and even arrested for assaulting his wife. Although he became a sports broadcaster he never found a purpose to replace his football career.

This is an example of what can happen if we don't have a sense of purpose in our lives. It makes us more vulnerable to boredom, anxiety and depression. And if we have an addictive personality it can make us vulnerable to substance abuse.

On the other hand, having a strong sense of purpose can have a powerful positive effect. When you have a purpose, getting up in the morning is never a problem. Life becomes easier, less complicated and less stressful.

A powerful example again comes from Viktor Frankl's book, *Man's Search for Meaning*[19], in which he describes his experiences in concentration camps during the Second World War. He observed that the inmates who were most likely to survive were those who managed to retain a sense of purpose.

Perhaps the most important questions any of us has to answer are: Why am I here? What do I really want to do with my life? Why am I doing what I do? What is my purpose? This question is important, not only in the larger scheme of life, but also in relation to smaller goals and even daily behaviour: "Why am I doing what I'm doing?"

We don't get burned out because of what we do; we get burned out because we forget why we're doing it.

That's why Purpose is at the tip of the Arrowhead. It gives meaning to our journey, sharpens our focus and gives us the strength to carry on when the going gets tough.

Figure 5.2: Purpose

I've always known purpose was important but it was really highlighted for me in 2003.

At that stage I was consulting in the USA six to eight times a year. I'd been asked to facilitate a meeting of a particular Young Presidents' Organisation forum in Florida. They'd heard I facilitated 'dialogue groups'... meetings where a particular topic could be thoroughly discussed leading to a good understanding of the topic, and if necessary, action being taken to achieve any change needed.

I arrived at the meeting to find eight individuals ready and eager to begin. First everyone introduced themselves giving a really thorough introduction covering both personal and business aspects of their lives. What surprised me most was how each one described, using numbers, exactly how wealthy they were. They all owned or managed highly profitable businesses, which was clearly reflected in the lifestyles they described. Numerous homes in desirable locations, boats, jets, cars, travel to exotic places, exclusive club memberships – they certainly had it all.

When we finished the introductions, I suggested we brainstorm a list of topics to discuss and then prioritise them with the most important ones discussed first.

They had come prepared and told me there was only one topic they wanted to thoroughly discuss. I asked them what it was and their answer bowled me over.

"We want to know why we're all so desperately unhappy!"
Powerful, honest discussion followed, and it lasted the whole day.

*Every one of them could remember why they started their business. The **powerful** purpose of building something meaningful, the challenge of building something great, and yes, also the goal of creating wealth, were all key drivers.*

After much soul searching they agreed that as much as they wanted the wealth, the enthusiasm and energy that came from their purpose was what really fired them up. The challenge of achievement. The building of something of value. The sense of accomplishment. A keen vision of the life they were trying to create for themselves and their families. This was what kept them awake at night with anticipatory excitement, and provided them with the desire to carry on in those inevitable moments of doubt when hurdles seemed insurmountable and energy was low.

As they discussed these hurdles, the question arose, "What kept you going? Why didn't you throw the towel in?" And the answer came like a bolt out the blue, loud and clear. "It wasn't the thought of the money that kept me going, no. I wasn't prepared to let myself or my family down. I wasn't prepared to let this get the better of me. That's what kept me going."

At the end of the day, it wasn't about me versus the money. No, it was about 'Me vs. Me', and they were not prepared to let themselves down. Yes – the money was the score line, the much wanted result, but the real motivation to do what needed to be done came from within. If money really had sufficient power to motivate then everyone would be achieving more, because most people want more money. Money is a score. Money is an outcome. Money is a result.

A powerful lesson

And so they slowly built their businesses, with the financial reward always top of mind. Yet on reflection they agreed money was only the score line that measured how well they were doing, and yes, they had their financial goals, but they also accepted that money was not the real motivator. The real fuel that drove their performance was their purpose; to build a great successful business; to achieve something worthwhile, something to be proud of. To look in the mirror and know that, 'I did it.' Through the discussion each one eventually discovered what their individual purpose was. What drove them to do what they did? Each one eventually realised and connected with the higher meaning that fuelled their motivation.

Was building a business stressful? Yes, but they all described the stress as being positive and motivating. They also described themselves as being happy at that stage. They were making meaningful progress. The key word – meaningful. They were living out their purpose, which had great personal meaning. Their arrow was in full flight.

As the day went on we heard stories of how much harder it was to achieve success than they had imagined. How much longer it took to reach profitability; how much more capital was required than their business plan provided for. We heard about the incredibly long hours they put in as their businesses struggled to move from surviving to thriving, which eventually happened.

What they described was clear. It was above the line personal accountability. As they encountered the many unpredictable hurdles and challenges on their journey, rather than play the blame game and feel sorry for themselves, they gave so many examples of living above the line. Becoming creative; finding solutions; the support they received from others and the constant learning that happened along the way. And it was their purpose which kept them above the line. A strong sense of purpose is a powerful way to ensure you live above the line. Without meaningful motivation, it's easy to slip below the line.

Yet as their businesses became profitable and their wealth grew, they became ensnared by a few subtle success traps.

They shifted their focus from purpose to profit. What kept them awake at night was no longer the excitement of building something great, but the challenge of how to ensure profit growth in the next fiscal. They shifted their focus from important long-term purpose to short-term results, and in this quest, as often happens, they lost sight of their purpose.

They shifted their focus from the Arrowhead to the target!

They all agreed that they had more fun, excitement and enjoyment in the early days of building their business than they had now trying to ensure ongoing profitability. In order to recapture the excitement and motivation of the early purpose driven days, they had all tried investing in other businesses and the resulting losses when we added them up were in the millions. Why? The intention was money driven, not purpose driven. As you'll see as the Leadership arrow unfolds, if they had gone beyond the scorecard of money and connected with 'why' they wanted to do this, their quest would have been infused with the power of purpose and the outcome might have been so very different.

> *"It's fine to climb a mountain – if that's your vision – so you can experience the view. It's not ok to climb the mountain so that everyone can look at you!"*
>
> Unknown

Figure 5.3: The power of 'And'

In business, when profit becomes the purpose, it's easy to introduce business practices that maximise short-term profit, which can often cause longer-term damage to the business. These short-term practices, when introduced, more often than not cause great personal stress because of the negative outcomes on other important variables like trust, people, and a healthy working environment. The way many cope is to keep telling themselves it's in the best interests of the business, but it's not. It's in the best interests of short-term profit and many owners/managers have to live in the long-term with the personal stress this short-term focus causes.

Sure, they're maximising profit, but they wonder why they feel so uneasy… if profit comes at the expense of purpose, then as profits go up, side effects creep in and stress levels can dramatically increase.

Like so many situations, the short-term profit goal and the longer-term sustainability issue are seemingly at loggerheads with each other. They are polarities, opposites – and as with all polarities the challenge is in the balance. It's not EITHER/OR but what I call the 'Power of AND.' It's the ability to find a way forward that favours neither one polarity nor the other, but that legitimises both and finds creative solutions that move the situation to an even greater level of value creation than the sum of the two opposites.

Profit and sustainability should be value-adding partners, not value-destroying competitors.

As an example, one can have a passion for deal making that results in massive profit. This success might appear to be money driven but if you look beyond the profit you'll see the key motivator – a passion for deal making. As so many successfully wealthy individuals have said to me, "I love doing the deal – it's what drives me. It's my purpose, that's what I was born to do."

Purpose and the three psychological stages of money

The first stage is NEED. To have enough money to support ourselves at a very basic level; to put food in our stomachs, clothes on our backs and a roof over our heads. At this level, survival can be a purpose. However, for the majority of readers of this book and for those who have adequate paying jobs, the quest for survival can't be a powerful purpose. If you're earning adequately and find yourself still being driven by a survival purpose, then ask yourself this question:

Survival for the sake of what?

The second stage kicks in when we have enough money to satisfy our basic needs and we start upgrading our lives with the better things that we desire and can afford. There's nothing wrong with this. Mincemeat is replaced with fillet steak. Our clothing needs to be branded and the roof over our head should be in a particular suburb. In this stage, external possessions become a motivator, and sure they can energise and move people to higher levels of achievement. The problem arises when the need to acquire becomes an addiction, acquisition is driven by greed, and we never arrive at a place of contentment.

A typical indicator that you're in the stage of greed is when you're not able to fully enjoy something you've worked for and achieved because you're already thinking of the next goal. You're sitting on the beach on the long awaited and worked hard for holiday, and rather than fully enjoy the moment, you're planning the next holiday in your mind. There's always something better you're working towards. This is a condition that contradicts a state of happiness. It's a form of addiction. We're hooked and need a regular fix, but the withdrawal symptoms will set in and the need for the next fix will often drive destructive behaviour, until eventually, one day, we look in the mirror and ask, "Why am I so unhappy – look at everything I've got?" There's no other outcome if you allow stage two acquisition to become greed.

Given that many people are wealthier today than at any time in history, there's clearly a marked difference between being 'well off' and 'wellbeing.'

Add purpose into the mix and acquisition or greed moves to the third stage of money, FREED. Here we let go of money as the primary source of our motivation. We don't do what we do for the money. We do what we do because we love it. It's our purpose. Our passion. We're above the line. And the most amazing thing happens. People who are freed, whether company employed or self-employed, often make more money than those living in greed. Think about it. Who's going to deliver a better service or product?

Would it be someone who's driven by the greed motive, or someone who does it for higher reasons? Who would you rather be dealing with? Who do you think makes more sustainable profit in the end? Whose career do you think grows fastest?

Our purpose is our soul...money is our goal.

Soul + Goal = Sustainable success

After a recent, successful back operation I developed an innocent synovial cyst on my spine. The problem was that it was pressing on a nerve in my spinal column causing pain in my leg. The neuro-surgeon who did the original operation arranged for me to have this cyst drained by a doctor in Johannesburg, who, for professional reasons, I will refer to as Dr S. He told me Dr S was world-class in carrying out this procedure. When I updated my GP and my physician as to what was going to happen, my GP commented that I was in excellent hands as Dr S was probably one of the best in the world. My physician stated that Dr S was regarded as number one in this field. After I had undergone the procedure, I mentioned to Dr S the comments I'd received about him and asked why he does what he does? He pointed to a wall that was papered with letters from patients who he'd helped and said, "That's why I do what I do!", and after a pause added, "And the money... is a bonus."

Another similar example was an accidental meeting during a business trip to New York in 2011.

One evening my wife and I went to Del Frisco's restaurant for dinner. Although the food was superb, the highlight of the evening was definitely the incredible service we received from a young waitress, Jennifer Sin. I wondered why she asked me for my business card and found out on our return to South Africa when I was really surprised to get a handwritten note from her thanking us for our patronage and for giving her the privilege of serving us.

A few months later, on a return visit to New York, we again went to Del Frisco's and this time we asked specifically to be served by Jennifer. After I complimented her on the handwritten note and her superb service I asked her what motivated her to deliver such incredible service. Her answer: "Opera." She told me she had a passion for singing opera and after studying at The Boston Conservatoire of

Music she came to New York looking for an opportunity to launch her career in opera. She went to auditions daily hoping for a part, but to date had little success. She knew however that her opportunity would come and didn't regard her waitressing job only as a means of supporting herself, but rather as part of her journey to fulfil her purpose.

I must stress a point. There's nothing wrong with the desire to make as much money as possible. There's nothing wrong with wanting to own or experience the many wonderful things money can buy. Each of us is free to set whatever level of goal or lifestyle we choose.

In business, the same applies. There's nothing wrong with wanting to make as much profit as you can. In fact, ongoing revenue and profit growth are signs of a healthy and sustainable business, but:

> The organisation's purpose should be its prime powerful motivation as the business travels towards its objectives and results.

The defining yet subtle difference between greed and freed lies in the prime intention.

In greed the intention sits in the Shaft; it's money. In freed the intention is in the Arrowhead; it's purpose and the result is money.

The power of Purpose in business

When an organisation is injected with purpose, employee engagement soars, retention increases, productivity is multiplied and profits are the result.

"If you're not in business to change people's lives, what are you doing?"

Robbie Brozin – Co-founder and former CEO: Nando's[20]

In the 1990s Boeing's grip on the world's aviation market made it the most powerful market leader in world business. Boeing's purpose was airplanes.

CEO Bill Allen said, "The spirit of myself and my colleagues is to eat, breathe and sleep the world of aeronautics." They created the 737, the most successful passenger airliner in history. When a non-executive director asked for details of the expected return on investment he was brushed off – some studies had been made… There were positive indications but Allen couldn't remember the details. He just enthused about how the plane would fly.

By the early 1990s Boeing had established total dominance in the world of civil aviation. Boeing created the most commercially successful aircraft company – not through love of profit but through love of planes. The oblique approach to profitability delivered spectacular results. An acquisition of McDonnell Douglas was followed by a decisive shift in corporate culture. New CEO Phil Condit: "We are going into a value based environment where unit cost, return on development and shareholder return are the measures by which you will be judged."

Market verdict. The share price rose from USD32 to USD59 within weeks. By the time of his forced resignation in December 2013 the share price had fallen to under USD30. His successors again focused on the love of flying and by 2008 Boeing was back as a leader.

Merck Pharmaceuticals: "We try never to forget that medicine is for people, it's not for profits. The profits follow, and if we have remembered that, they never failed to appear. The better we have remembered that, the larger they have been." In 1995 a new CEO stated that Merck's number one objective was to be a top tier growth company. "As a company Merck is totally focused on growth."

Merck fell off Fortune's list of most admired companies.

Johnson & Johnson: "We believe our first responsibility is to the doctors, nurses and patients, to mothers and fathers and all others who use our products and services. When we align with this purpose the stockholders should realise a fair return."

The 702 Story: Channel 702, as it was originally called, was started by businessman Issie Kirsh in the 1980s to provide a platform for South Africans to talk to each other. Creating vibrant dialogue around any issue is the only way of understanding it and creating change. Issie Kirsh believed giving people this opportunity to communicate could bring about much needed change in South African politics.

The radio station was situated in the then homeland of Bophuthatswana, which was independent of South African rules and regulations. Because of its narrative it would never have been allowed to exist in suppressed South Africa. 702's purpose – to be In Touch, In Tune and Independent, and make a difference. People could talk freely about issues and openly share viewpoints. Wherever possible both sides of an opinion were aired. Apartheid was challenged. South Africans mind-sets were challenged. The possibility of a different future was openly discussed. By any business measure 702 was a highly successful radio station and driven by its purpose to be independent; it made profit.

In 1994 with the advent of the new democratic SA, the renamed Talk Radio 702's narrative changed. With the demise of apartheid, 702 had seemingly lost its purpose and went off in numerous directions. Both listenership and profits tumbled until the question was asked, "Is it time to shut down?" At that point Terry Volkwyn was the manager of 94.7 Highveld Stereo – also in the Primedia Broadcasting stable. She asked the board to give her a chance to resurrect 702 and they agreed.

In a subsequent strategy workshop I introduced the senior management team to some research on iconic brands, indicating that these brands had survived a period of seemingly getting lost through brand dilution, just as 702 had, but came back strongly and successfully through refocusing on their purpose. The initial comment was that with the demise of apartheid 702 had lost its rallying point. Further discussion, however, brought the realisation that although apartheid no longer existed, the purpose, 'To make a difference', was still valid.

Democracy brought with it a new set of challenges, such as education, crime, health care, etc., and 702 could be a catalyst for making a difference by encouraging active citizenship. Out of this thinking came the highly successful LeadSA vision and strategy.

TOMS

In 2006, American traveller, Blake Mycoskie, befriended children in a village in Argentina where he noticed the hardships of going through life without shoes. Wanting to help he created TOMS, a company that would match every pair of shoes purchased with a pair of new shoes given to a child in need. 'One for One' was born. To date, TOMS has given 35 million pairs of shoes to children in need in over 60 countries. Blake didn't start a business, he started a movement, and needless to say his business is thriving.

GARY PLAYER

The iconic golfer, Gary Player, once said he wants his epitaph to read, *"Here is a man who was interested in his fellow man – and in education and health. And he bettered the lives of poor people."* A lofty purpose, certainly. But as he walked out of the clubhouse of the Augusta National after a long morning of signatures, handshakes and television interviews and undoubtedly a large cheque, Player said, "Ok! Made another million friends – wasn't that nice!" And he meant it. A man truly driven by purpose.

"When the call is heeded with full commitment and conscious engagement, then the execution will shine with fire and luminous brightness. Through passion and intensity our work will be a blissful pleasure; and instinctual gratification, if you will."

Dr Deon van Zyl – Clinical Psychologist; Management, Training and Development Consultant.

Why am I here…?

This is the most important question to answer before we can lead ourselves and others.

It's the tip of the Leadership Arrow.

So, why are you here? Obviously there's a lot riding on your answer. It's not only about your own life or business, but also the lives of everyone else you or your organisation will affect in your lifetime. You could choose to be insignificant, but you might also choose to play a hugely significant role in the future direction of your life, of others' lives, of your country, and even of the planet. Conscious choice gives you that option. The option of living above or below the line. Above the line is about accountability. Being responsible for living your purpose is the ultimate accountability.

However, as you begin tackling this question, there's a good chance you'll find it such a daunting task that you'll soon yield to the temptation of returning to your comfort zone. Please don't do that. Although this question is one of the major challenges you'll face as a human being and a leader, it's a question each one of us must and can answer, and it's well worth the effort.

If you don't know what your purpose is, then finding it is your purpose for now.

Is finding your purpose an event? No, it's a process. It's a never-ending quest, and the answer to the question could change as life or business evolves. Purpose is not discovered once and then we are done with it; it's re-examined at various points in our lives, typically during crises and major transitions.

Understanding and living your purpose is fundamental for being happy, but simply being in the process of searching for your purpose can achieve the same thing.

Is it possible to be happy 24/7? The answer is no. However the more time you spend being yourself, the more fulfilled you'll feel, the happier you'll be and the more you'll achieve.

My personal journey

For so many of my early adult years I really thought I knew what my purpose was, yet something was missing in my life. I suppose the best way to describe it was to say I kept 'pushing' in order to succeed, resulting in excessive tiredness, even reaching the level of burnout on the odd occasion. But I was achieving my goals and wasn't that what it was all about? I had studied the subject of purpose in my university curriculum and I suppose I was arrogant enough to think that was enough.

As time went on I started to feel my motivation waning, my enthusiasm declining and started experiencing a reluctance to sit at my desk and work. There was no fun any more in what I was doing, even though I was achieving goals, and this state spilled over into all areas of my life and into everything I did. I started questioning who I was and especially what I was doing, trying so many different approaches in my role as a consultant, looking for the silver bullet that would re-energise me.

On a trip to the USA I came across a unique bookstore in San Diego that specialised in personal development and organisational development resources and spent two full days in that store pouring through unique book after book. These were the days before the Internet, so access to this kind of information was limited. I spent my whole travel budget on two huge boxes of books and shipped them back to South Africa. If these kinds of resources were scarce even in regular bookshops in the USA, in South Africa at that time they were non-existent.

When the books arrived I was like a child on a birthday, confronted by mounds of gifts and not knowing which one to open first. The signs of my purpose were there even though I didn't realise it at the time: learning, growth, development, people in business. I was excited. I hardly slept for days on end as I poured through all this information. This started my habit of using my early wake up time of 4am to read for one and a half hours every day – something I still do today. Out of this developed part of my philosophy for dealing with my clients: "If my client hears about it and it's relevant to their business, then they need to hear it from me first."

In one of the books I purchased I came across a few structured exercises for defining your purpose. For the first time I was staring my purpose in the face – it was there for me to see. As normally happens, the description of my purpose took some time to crystallise and went through numerous iterations.

My purpose is to be a source of inspiration and a catalyst of growth. This is the tip of my Arrowhead. It's the emotional fuel that energises me. Am I perfect? Emphatically, no! Sometimes life, pressure, deadlines, challenges and hurdles start getting to me and then I slip into resentment, but at those times I have learned to centre myself back on my purpose, giving me the intrinsic motivation and strength to move forward positively.

Just in case I've given the wrong message about money and material possessions, let me say I love having nice things, enjoying great experiences, having a lovely home, travelling, and building the required wealth to provide these and more for myself and my family. These are goals I set for myself. They are not my purpose, **but living my purpose means I really enjoy what I do and makes it possible, and even most likely,** for me to achieve my goals and to have all these things.

"Let wealth be the result of your work, not the purpose of it."

Ted Coine: Chief Relationship Officer, Meddle.it

How to find your personal purpose

So much has been written on how to find your purpose and all this information is as close as a Google search. There are, however, some suggestions common to most approaches and these provide a good starting point.

Begin with the following three exercises:

Exercise

1. Write the answers down and look for common themes.

    ➤ Identify three situations, in different parts of your life including your career, when you have been particularly happy. For each situation, write down what it was about those situations that made you feel happy. Try to identify up to three factors for each situation.

    ➤ Now repeat this exercise by looking at situations in which you have felt particularly proud of something you have done. Again, identify three situations and identify the factors that contributed to your pride in each situation.

    ➤ Analyse your answers for common themes that made you feel good and energised when you read them.

    ➤ Think about these themes during your incubation time.

These answers will help you in Exercise 3.

2.   Answering the following questions will also help you to connect with your purpose.

➤   What do you want people to say about you at your funeral?

➤   What makes you come alive?

➤   What are your innate strengths and talents?

➤   What would you do for free for the rest of your life if you were a billionaire?

➤   Whose life would you love to have lived? Why?

➤   How will you measure your life?

➤   Analyse your answers. Again do you see any common themes? Write these down.

These answers will also help you in Exercise 3.

3.   Read the following and answer the question.

➤   You can't discover your purpose from a viewpoint of your comfort zone; it's best done in an environment that's not part of your daily routine. People are creatures of habit and unless you move away from what you're used to, your mind will be limited by old thinking. You need to be in an environment where you find it easy to be in the moment, where you can be with yourself and without the usual distractions that will pull your mind elsewhere. Some people need to get away totally to a place of peace and quiet. Nothing, just you. Some people find being out in nature provides this. A method that works well and has many other advantages which I can personally recommend, is to learn and practice a relaxation or meditation technique. The modern approach to Mindfulness is also hugely effective. All are easily available either in book form, online or in training courses.

➤   Once you're in a conducive environment take a few minutes to reread and reflect on your answers from Exercises 1 and 2, and then take out a blank sheet of paper or use your PC or tablet and answer the following question:

What is my true purpose in life?

Your answer doesn't have to be a complete sentence; a short phrase is fine. Repeat this step until you find an answer that triggers off an emotional reaction. This is your purpose. That's it. To some people this exercise will make perfect sense. To others it will seem utterly stupid. Usually it takes 15-20 minutes to clear your head of all the clutter and the social conditioning about what you think your purpose in life is. The false answers will come from your mind and your memories. But when the true answer finally arrives, it will feel like it's coming to you from a different source entirely. As you go through this process, some of your answers will be very similar. You may even re-list previous answers but that's okay. Keep going. When you find your own unique answer to the question of why you're here, you'll feel it resonate with you deeply. The words will seem to have a special energy and you'll feel that energy whenever you read them. Discovering your purpose is the easy part. The hard part is keeping it with you on a daily basis and working on yourself to the point where you become that purpose. The final chapter will deal with leading yourself through your purpose.

Finding your business purpose

"Purpose expresses the company's fundamental value – the raison d'être or overriding reason for existing. It is the end to which the strategy is directed."

Richard Ellsworth[21]

Many businesses understand what their purpose – the tip of their Leadership Arrow – is. Some businesses know how to live and lead with purpose, creating incredible organisational passion and motivation.

Steve Jobs' mission statement for Apple in 1980 was: "To make a contribution to the world by making tools for the mind that advance humankind."[22]

Unfortunately, for many businesses a purpose is no more than an idealistic statement in a document or on a wall. A later chapter will suggest how to use organisational purpose as a powerful Leadership tool.

Finding a business or departmental purpose is possibly a little more difficult than thinking about an individual purpose. It needs patience and a thorough facilitated discussion to arrive at a purpose statement that is understood and committed to by all key stakeholders. Most CEOs pay lip service to the idea of purpose. After all, it's not how they're measured. It's not one of their key performance indicators or a balanced scorecard metric.

When LeadSA was proposed at a Primedia Broadcasting strategy workshop as the vehicle for living out its purpose of 'To make a difference', it resulted in a full day's heated debate. Resources would have to be allocated to the initiative. Was it worth it? The board wanted to know what the return on the investment would be? How could it be monetised? It couldn't. It was Primedia Broadcasting's purpose. It was the tip of their Arrowhead. It would focus the total business on its purpose, building meaning and energising the organisation. It would also add positive value to the individual radio station brands.

It would send a message telling the market who Primedia Broadcasting was and what it stood for. It wasn't just another successful and profitable business. It would be the kind of business advertisers and listeners wanted to be associated with and would want to support. It would be the kind of business people wanted to work for. It would give the business 'soul.' As this 'soul' of the business developed, so it became a brand in its own right and one of the fastest growing brands in South Africa. It says loud and clear that Primedia Broadcasting stands for more than just brilliant radio and making profit. Is LeadSA for sale in any way or format? I should think not.

➤ Is it possible to have 'soul' if you don't have a purpose…? No.

➤ Would you sell your soul?

➤ If you did, what would happen to your credibility?

➤ Would anyone want to follow you?

NO PURPOSE
This is why PURPOSE sits at the tip
of the Leadership Arrow.
Without it the arrow is blunt.
Without it Leadership is stunted.

Figure 5.4: Blunt Arrow

Get into the habit of constantly asking yourself, especially in difficult times:

"Why am I doing this?" The answer will make you strong.

To finish off this chapter, I would like to share a letter I received during March 2015 from Gela Ohl, Marketing Manager at TAL, a division of Norcros SA, which is one of my clients. It is a perfect illustration of the journey towards finding your purpose.

Finding my purpose

Words have always fascinated me. It excites me when I come across a new word or read a beautiful poem. I enjoy reading and crafting great copy. I am also truly happy when I travel, exploring new places and cultures and expanding my world view. I have 25 years' experience in marketing and even though I find it stimulating, dynamic and very rewarding, I have reached a point where I am questioning as to whether I want to do this for the rest of my life. To be honest, the prospect depresses me. My contemporaries are much younger than I am and I find I no longer become as excited about the next campaign as they do. Years of practice in marketing developed my writing and editing skills and entrenched my love of language. I started contemplating alternative careers. I was looking for something that I could do which combined my love of language with my love of travel, but nothing suitable came to mind.

Then, one day, a friend mentioned that she is planning to travel the world and teach English when she retires. A light went on for me. I remembered that I had always wanted to teach but instead had decided on a career in commerce.

I researched some options and enrolled in a Teaching English to Speakers of Other Languages (TESOL) course at a language school. I enjoyed the course and did well but had no idea how I would apply it once I graduated. I reasoned that some of the skills would probably come in handy when preparing future marketing campaigns and the teaching aspect would have to wait until I retired. A few months went by and I received a phone call from the language school asking whether I would be interested in teaching a small class of second language English speakers on a part-time basis. I agreed and discovered that I LOVED IT. It was a rewarding and humbling experience. Soon I was teaching a second intake and a third intake and the more I taught, the more rewarding the experience became. Nothing comes close to the satisfaction of seeing a student gain confidence and start using the language you have taught them. Currently I'm preparing to teach a course on English for Marketing and I'm thinking: "Does it get any better than this? The opportunity to combine my marketing skills with my teaching skills." Slowly it dawned on me that teaching adults is what I'm meant to do. It makes me happy and it is my purpose. I enrolled for a degree on a part-time basis at university and have begun the process of retraining into a second career.

For me, finding my purpose was not a sudden flash of inspiration but rather a journey of self-discovery and giving myself permission to "have-a-go." As I write this I'm still working full-time in marketing and I do not have a clear-cut vision as to where this will lead to. I have no specific goals, only a steadfast drive to focus and head in this direction, gaining as much experience as possible until I find a niche in this field. In the meantime, I am enjoying every moment and keeping an open mind.

Thank you Gela!

"Vision is the star we steer by. Everything begins with vision, everything flows from vision."

Frances Hesselbein[23]

Chapter 6

WHERE – LEADERSHIP CANNOT EXIST WITHOUT VISION

"Vision is a source of hope; it's a source of courage; it's the source of perseverance in the midst of difficulty."

Myles Munroe[24]

A fter purpose, vision is the next part of the Arrowhead. Where purpose answers the question: "Why am I here?", vision answers the question: "Where am I going?" Vision is a mental image of what your purpose would look like when it's turned into a living reality.

Figure 6.1: Vision

Story

Mike Vance, the first dean of Disney University, tells of a time when Walt Disney walked into his office in Disneyland and asked him what he was doing. "I'm working", Mike replied. "What does it look like I'm doing..?"

"That's not what I mean", Walt replied. "I'm wondering how come you're working when it's raining outside. You shouldn't be working, you should be outside walking in the rain."

So Walt convinces Mike to go walking in the rain. They're walking down Main Street, USA, an authentically recreated Main Street USA from 110 years ago, when Walt stops outside a shop with little cottage pane windows and asks, "Mike, what do those windows remind you of?"

"I don't know", replies Mike.

"Don't they remind you of the windows we all had in our homes when we were children?"

"Sure", Mike replies, saying he could remember his parent's home having similar cottage pane windows.

"Do you remember how as children we used to look out of those windows on rainy days like this and watch people running for cover?"

"I do", replies Mike.

"And do you remember how, as children, we used to stare into space and dream about the wonderful things we were going to do as adults?"

"Sure, I can remember that."

Then Walt said, "Isn't it wonderful to be an adult today and still be able to remember that child you were then?"

Mike: "Yes, that's wonderful."

Walt: "But Mike how much more wonderful to be an adult today, to still be able to remember that child you were then, and to know that you're busy achieving every single thing that child ever hoped and dreamed you would achieve?"

Mike: "Yes that's truly wonderful."

Walt: "Mike do you know what that's called... that's called success!"

"If you can dream it you can do it."

Walt Disney[25]

The problem of course, is the tramp saying things like:

> ➤ "I'll never be able to."
> ➤ "I don't have the qualifications."
> ➤ "Let's focus on more urgent priorities."
> ➤ "We don't have the budget."
> ➤ "I can do this in the new year."
> ➤ "As soon as the kids are educated..."
> ➤ "I'll do it tomorrow."

The trouble is... tomorrow never comes...

Being immobilised by the time trap

Our lives are made of our yesterdays, todays and tomorrows. The reality is that yesterday's negative, emotionally-laden experience often limits what we dream about for our future and results in us being immobilised today.

We get upset about stuff that's already happened and is now history, while we simultaneously worry about the future. These negative thoughts lead to negative emotions which crowd out any chance we have of acting constructively today and operating fully in the moment. Because we're immobilised in this way, not doing anything today to create the future we'd like to have, it leads to continued worrying, procrastination and addictive compensatory behaviour.

We overindulge, under exercise and become couch potatoes, watching a never ending stream of TV programmes transporting us into a world we wish we could have, a life we wish we could live. We even revert to drugs.

It's the only way we can survive. Our compensatory lifestyle becomes a coping addiction rather than life enhancing, and we're always looking for the next fix.

It's a never-ending downward spiral that can lead to mental and physical illness.

Alternatively we try to be positive and just put our head down and push forward by working as hard as possible, to ensure success and happiness. The result – a lack of focus, wasted energy and burnout. "Why am I so unhappy?" Fertile ground for the tramp.

It's almost like our past is an anchor that limits our chances of moving forward. Our past experience sets the thermostat level for our future achievement. Our past experience is like a governor on the accelerator of a high performance motor vehicle; it limits the speed at which it can travel.

Being immobilised by the time trap is one of the biggest causes of mediocre performance or even failure in individuals and in business. Because of past circumstances a below the line culture develops: people covering their butts, playing the blame game, feeling like victims, and in the process losing sight of their vision and their future.

Being immobilised by success

It's also possible that past success could make us resist challenging an approach which might have worked yesterday but certainly isn't appropriate for today. And isn't it true how when something isn't working it's so easy to get into denial and defend it by justifying it and referring to past success? Remember the first rule of holes? 'If you find yourself in a hole, stop digging.'

Note the demise of Kodak: they somehow couldn't see a vision of themselves in the digital era. They were stuck deep in a hole created by their incredible past success.

The problem, however, is that to stop digging you must first realise you're in a hole, and denial so often blinds us to this possibility. In fact the tramp can often get us into denial by making us feel as if we're not responsible for being in the hole. The following poem by Portia Nelson beautifully illustrates the tramp at work keeping us below the line in the victim loop – 'it's not my fault' – and then the moment of moving above the line into the accountability loop.

There is a hole in my sidewalk

(Reproduced with kind permission from Beyond Words Publishing, Hillsboro, Oregon.[26])

I
I walked down the street.
There is a deep hole in the sidewalk
I fall in.
I am lost ... I am helpless.
It isn't my fault.
It takes me forever to find a way out.

II
I walk down the same street.
There is a deep hole in the sidewalk.
I pretend I don't see it.
I fall in again.
I can't believe I am in the same place
but, it isn't my fault.
It still takes a long time to get out.

III
I walk down the same street.
There is a deep hole in the sidewalk.
I see it there.
I still fall in ... it's a habit.
My eyes are open
I know where I am.
It is my fault.
I get out immediately.

IV
I walk down the same street.
There is a deep hole in the sidewalk.
I walk around it.

V
I walk down another street.

And so it doesn't matter how much you've achieved in your life, if you're in a comfort zone created by past success or fear of the future, you could very well find yourself in a hole, limiting future growth.

This is the tramp at work... at his absolute best.

Our past is not our future

We need to keep telling ourselves this over and over until the message sinks into our subconscious. This is so important if we are to weaken the anchor of our past. Sure, the past is a phenomenal learning experience. It teaches us valuable lessons we can use in the next part of our journey. I am, however, aware that some people's pasts have really painful memories. Memories the tramp uses as a great excuse to stay in their comfort zone and prevent them from further hurt. It's not my intention to minimise these experiences. I urge you to see them for what they are, learn from them, and move on. If you can't self-manage them please seek professional help. It's worth it.

Three important words to remember: 'Life moves on.' The big question is... WHERE TO?

The first step for getting out of the trap of the past is to see a new, improved and meaningful tomorrow; to create a clear and desirable vision of the future.

And the first step for any individual or business that wants to seriously change the status quo is a clear vision of where he/it wants to be.

And any vision for tomorrow that is different to the status quo of today implies change.

The Pleasure/Pain principle

People will change for two reasons and two reasons only: when they see the light or when they feel the heat. This is the Pleasure/Pain principle. Human beings are always motivated to move towards pleasure and away from pain.

What the tramp does is highlight all the pain you might have to go through, including risk of failure, if you pursue a lofty vision, and then the tramp highlights the pleasure of staying in your comfort zone, even if it's not ideal.

This is why leaders with vision usually face serious resistance from other important stakeholders who, being influenced by their own tramps, become naysayers, highlighting all the reasons the leader's vision will fail.

This is why so often a person stays in an abusive relationship. They think of the insecurity of leaving the relationship (pain) and focus on the few benefits they get from staying in the relationship (pleasure).

Leaders switch it around, spelling out the brutal reality of the current situation to ensure discomfort, and then giving hope by creating and sharing a powerful and inspiring vision of what is possible, a vision that others want to be part of.

The tension trap

The very act of committing to a vision implies getting out of your comfort zone and embarking on a journey you've never been on before. Even the thought of this can cause most people great psychological tension. Yes, you might have to take a few risks and at times be uncomfortable. The rule book for your quest might not yet have been written and you'll write it over and over again.

> *"Life is like playing a violin solo in public and learning the instrument as one goes along."*
>
> Samuel Butler[27]

> *"If you want to walk on the water you've got to be prepared to step out of the boat."*
>
> John Ortberg[28]

Imagine a pole representing where you currently are; your comfort zone. Now imagine a pole out in your future, representing your vision, dream or goal. Imagine an elastic band between the two poles. The further the poles are apart, the tighter the elastic band stretches and the more tension that's created and experienced. This is the psychological tension created when we set goals that take us out of our comfort zone.

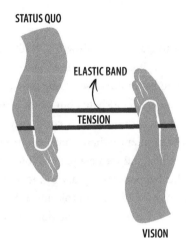

Figure 6.2: Psychological tension created when we set goals

A comfort zone is an area of competence surrounded by fear.

When you commit to a vision/goal (the future) that takes you out of your comfort zone (the past), the tension this causes will need to resolve itself. How? The pole that's more entrenched will pull the other less anchored pole towards it, reducing the tension.

Our past is usually so anchored by fear of leaving our comfort zone, and our dreams and goals are so weakened by a lack of clarity and our lack of self-belief, that in most cases the past wins, pulling our desired vision back to a more mediocre, comfortable and less stressful version of our future. Eventually, without even realising it, our vision is swamped by present circumstances and relegated to the side lines – even forgotten.

At this point it's so easy to dip below the line and get into denial, kidding ourselves that we're happy in our comfort zones and believing we should be grateful for what we've got.

This potentially damages our self-belief even further, so we need to give ourselves viable and justifiable excuses for abandoning our vision. Wow, the tramp really does this well! And so, we get stuck where we are.

The problem

We were not designed to stand still. Growth is built into the physical and psychological DNA of the human condition. We're naturally attracted to want to move forward, to better ourselves, to be more, to achieve more, and to have more. Even as we consciously tell ourselves we're ok in our comfort zone, our subconscious need for growth is constantly pushing up into our consciousness. At those moments when it pushes through, it can smack us out of the comfort of denial and create a pain of intense dissatisfaction and unhappiness. When this happens it's so easy to move deeper below the line into the doom loop by playing the victim role and I think by now we should realise where that gets us. We're stuck in the downward spiral of the doom loop.

When I speak to groups of people about vision, whether it's in the context of individual lives, business or government, I always emphasise the following truth because I believe it's critical for each of us to accept:

> *"The poorest person in the world is a person without a dream."*

Myles Munroe[29]

Maybe you've never known what to do with your life? Or maybe you had a dream but lost it through discouraging circumstances or the busyness of day-to-day living. No matter how much money you have, if you don't have a clear vision for your life you are truly poor. As the saying goes: 'If you don't know where you're going, any road will get you there.' What's worse, you won't even know when you've arrived. Unless you have a definite idea of where you want to go, the chances of your getting there are remote.

The problem is that most people cannot see beyond their current circumstances.

➤ Without a meaningful vision of the future, life loses its meaning.

➤ An absence of meaning then leads to a lack of hope.

➤ People without hope can become resentful of their jobs or their families.

➤ They start living with a nagging internal longing for something more.

➤ They may even stop participating in life in a significant way.

No matter how much money a person might have, anyone who lives like this is poor. A visionless life is a poverty-stricken existence.

Is this you?

Are these your employees?

These people come to the end of their lives drained, not completed.

But remember we do have a choice. We can choose to go above the line into a growth cycle, **but to do this we must have a vision of where we're going. Our vision gives us powerful motivation for staying above the line.**

Staying above the line means accepting accountability for creating your life, but how is it possible to be accountable for creating anything if we don't have a powerful, clear, and meaningful vision of what it is? It's just not possible.

In 1995 I was asked by the YPO (Young President's Organisation) to design an experience suitable for about 25 members and their families. As members of YPO these individuals are privileged to be exposed to many exciting growth experiences during their tenure, so to create an experience is always a challenge... it needs to be both unique and a great learning experience. Eventually I decided to take them to Robben Island for a weekend. This was just after the 1994 democratic elections in SA when Robben Island was closed down as a prison but not yet opened up as a museum.

We arrived there at lunchtime on a Friday and left on Sunday afternoon. I had contacted ex-political prisoners who had spent time incarcerated on Robben Island and each family was allocated an ex-prisoner to be their guide and source of information for the weekend. The idea was that the families could hear first-hand what it was like to grow up in apartheid era South Africa;

how people became activists; what it was like at the hands of the police; the subsequent trials; and great detail about life as a prisoner on Robben Island.

It was the most amazing weekend of understanding, learning and mind-set changing.

In the early days a single cell didn't even have a bed in it but only a thin mattress on the floor. There was a toilet in the corner, a small metal cupboard for the few personal belongings you were allowed to have, and a large bucket of water, which was your water for washing and drinking. It was filled daily.

All the leaders of the ANC were imprisoned on Robben Island and although there was no communication allowed or tolerated regarding the anti-apartheid struggle, they managed to lead the country to democratic freedom. How did they manage this with no communication allowed?

Well, as we found out, despite this challenge there was in fact communication happening. We heard how at two o'clock in the morning when the prison was silent, prisoners would use a drinking cup to empty the toilet water into the empty water bucket. When the toilets were emptied, they made perfect channels of communication.

We also heard about the regular soccer games that were part of Robben Island life and how moves were played that communicated plans regarding the struggle. We were told how the third grade, very large loaves of bread (for the prisoners only) were delivered by ferry daily from a bakery on the mainland. These huge bread loaves were then cut into big chunks and distributed to prisoners as their daily bread rations. What the officials never found out was that there were notes baked into the crust of the bread.

How did they manage to pull this off? They had a powerful purpose and a vision that not only kept them going during the toughest of times, but also motivated them to look for creative solutions to their problems. Their vision gave them the strength to stay above the line and make proactive choices instead of going below the line, playing the blame game, and falling into the victim or doom loop.

Together purpose and vision give incredible focus to the arrow as it travels towards its target. In a later chapter you will see the powerful Leadership opportunity that this provides.

So what is your vision?

The first step to understanding your vision is to realise that it always emanates from your purpose.

> Purpose is when you know and understand what you were born to accomplish.

> Vision is when you can see it in your mind. When you begin to imagine what it looks like as you live out your purpose.

> When you're able to see your purpose, your vision comes to life.

Your vision may be clear to you or it may be buried somewhere deep inside you waiting to be discovered. The fundamental challenge of life is to find our purpose and vision and fulfil it. Until we do, we merely exist.

Vision is the strongest motivator of human behaviour; it influences what we do and what we don't do. It highlights our priorities and is a guide to how we live our lives. Vision provides the fuel of passion that we need to stay in and win this race called life.

Leadership without vision is just not possible!

Corporate vision

In my experience it's a fallacy to think that a larger corporate vision originates from a group; it's more often than not the case that a leader has the vision. The leader then shares their vision with the group and transfers it to them. The members of the group then run with the vision *because they find in it a place for their own personal visions to be fulfilled.*

Nelson Mandela had a vision of a free and democratic South Africa. When he shared his vision it tapped into something so many South Africans dreamed about. It hooked their visions and they followed him; they found a place for their own personal visions within his vision. This is an important idea for leaders to understand. It's the essence of why a vision has power. But note, it can't be selfish. If it is it will disconnect the followers from the leader.

The LeadSA vision of Primedia Broadcasting connected with every citizen's desire to create a better South Africa.

The 'One for One' vision of TOMS shoes connected with every employees' instinctive desire to help disadvantaged children.

Maybe now you can see why 'to be a billion dollar company' or 'to have 15% annual growth over the next 10 years' are not visions. Both are valid as objectives, but not visions. They don't connect and bring to the surface any personal vision or aspiration individuals might have.

A leader will dig deep into your being and begin to draw out what you're dreaming, thinking and desiring. He'll present the corporate vision and you'll become excited about participating in it because you'll see how your personal vision finds fulfilment in it.

South Africa's National Development Plan (NDP) is an excellent example of a powerful vision that digs deep into people's psyche and begins to draw out what they are thinking, dreaming and desiring.

Here is a condensed version of that vision. You can see the full vision at www.gov.za/issues/national-development-plan-2030.

South Africa belongs to all its peoples.

We, the people, belong to one another.

We live the rainbow.

Our homes, neighbourhoods, villages, towns, and cities are safe and filled with laughter.

Through our institutions, we order our lives.

The faces of our children tell of the future we have crafted.

Leaders understand reality and then through using the power of vision they give people hope.

Finding your personal vision

➤ Take half an hour and allow yourself to dream about what you would like to do in life. What ideas and desires do you have? What have you always wanted to do or have?

➤ Think about your primary talents and strengths. How do your dreams, talents and strengths go together?

➤ Write down your dreams, ideas, desires, talents and strengths and read them over every evening for a week. Then ask yourself, 'Do these ideas hold true?' 'Are they what I want to do?' If the answer is yes, keep them where you can refer to them and watch them form into a specific vision of your future that embodies everything that's important to you.

➤ Create a vision board to keep your vision top of mind until it's fully internalised. To do this simply cut out, from old magazines, pictures that depict the ideal life your vision represents and paste these meaningfully onto a poster board. Display it where it can be easily and frequently seen.

And ask yourself – do you remember the child you once were?

"**How do we successfully compete and achieve our vision, in an increasingly complex moment-to-moment world, delivering against short-term expectations on demand, in a sustainable way, we can feel good about?**"

Doug Conant and Mette Norgaard[30]

Chapter 7

HOW – LEADING THE WAY
THROUGH STRATEGY

S trategy sits at the base of the Arrowhead and performs the critical role of connecting the direction of the Arrowhead with the execution of the Shaft. Without a strategy the vision is nothing more than a dream. The strategy defines in broad terms how the vision is going to be achieved, and forms the basis of decision-making and behaviour in the execution process.

In the cut and thrust of changing daily demands and challenges it's so easy to get pulled in different directions, losing focus and dispersing limited resources and energy. Decisions are made based solely on short-term demands and needs – the so-called 'urgent' priorities of execution – while the longer term 'important' Leadership issues around purpose and vision and sustainability are neglected.

Figure 7.1: Strategy

A well-defined strategy will give a life or business the absolute focus that is so important for success. Note: we don't have unlimited energy or resources to achieve our ultimate vision or goals, so successful lives and businesses are focused. Strategy does for humans and business what blinkers do for horses – keeps them from being distracted.

The power of focus

Strategy has the same effect as the convex lens referred to in chapter 5. It focuses the energy, resulting in a greater impact and heightened chance of success. But of course it can't be just any strategy; it must be an appropriate and sustainable strategy.

Yet, as important as strategy is, ask the average middle manager or employee on whom the company depends to execute its strategy – "What's the business strategy?" and very few can answer. Think about it. If the majority of employees don't know the strategy, can the business claim to have one?

In the industrial age when most jobs were highly structured and efficiencies were managed by systems, processes and procedures, people were not required to think much but needed to follow well designed and efficient processes. Today, in an era where services are driving economies, businesses and jobs, the average day requires ongoing thinking, problem solving, innovation and decision-making to succeed, and these can't successfully exist in a highly structured and controlled environment.

To achieve the level of accountability and proactivity that is needed today takes engaged and empowered people who can make the right choices and decisions as problems and challenges present themselves, which can't be achieved through rules or a prescribed approach. People are unique and have diverse perspectives, opinions, individual agendas and goals to achieve, as determined by their job description or mandate or whatever they are incentivised for, as well as their own individual personal agendas.

Most senior executives will tell you their business does have a vision, but just because vision exists, it doesn't necessarily mean it's connected to the Shaft – the operations.

It takes something else to make that connection – strategy.

Strategy connects the vision in the Arrowhead to the execution in the Shaft.

While managers operating in the Shaft will generally focus on behaviour that achieves short-term objectives, leaders add meaning and empower people by constantly highlighting the connection between short-term objectives and the strategy of the business.

It's so easy for the strategy to become blurred or even lost in the journey from the Arrowhead to the behaviour in the Shaft; a journey encountering many hurdles and detours. A journey made difficult by:

➤ over complicated and detailed strategic plans

➤ inadequate strategy communication. Strategy is not just a message to be communicated; strategy is a story – a philosophy that must be understood if it's going to be lived. A story good leaders tell, creating understanding and commitment – one that 'sticks' and isn't easily forgotten. More about this in chapter 12

> ➤ reward and recognition metrics that create conflicting priorities. So often managers create milestones or metrics that create reward or punishment outcomes that drive behaviour not aligned with strategy. (A call centre I consulted for had 'Superior Customer Service' as a key strategic differentiator, and yet operators were measured and incentivised by the number of calls they dealt with hourly. You can imagine what happened to customer service…)

> ➤ the necessity of meeting unrealistic short-term budgets or goals often drives managers to make decisions which are potentially damaging to longer-term strategy. One client's management team decided to delay buying new vehicles and servicing existing trucks as one way of achieving their budget and ensuring their bonuses. Ongoing breakdowns impacted negatively on service delivery and results, and worse still, somebody was killed in an accident involving one of their unserviced trucks, subsequently found to be faulty.

And yet, as important as strategy is, these are comments I so frequently hear:

> ➤ We don't have a clear strategy.
> ➤ I don't understand the strategy.
> ➤ If we have a strategy they certainly don't communicate it to us.
> ➤ I don't believe in the strategy.
> ➤ They tell us the strategy but certainly don't act as if they're serious about it.
> ➤ How can they devise a strategy without understanding the reality of what we face executing it?
> ➤ They expect us to execute the strategy but they don't give us the budget and resources to do so.

Developing strategy

The purpose of this chapter isn't to suggest how to develop strategy. A whole book could be devoted to the understanding and process of arriving at good strategy. I don't think there's a business topic that's generated so many diverse opinions as strategy.

Academic theories abound. Processes for strategic planning are numerous. What constitutes good strategy is constantly debated, with new theories espoused regularly. This is probably because strategy is not a reactive, analytical process. Yes it requires a fair amount of analysis, but any final strategic decision is hugely intuitive, based on assumptions of what the environment and competition is going to be like in the future and applying our strengths to these.

This is the antithesis of what most managers are comfortable with. In the end it's a huge judgement call. How many CEOs have been exited for betting on poor strategies? Because of this inherent uncertainty companies tend to over-analyse, using once-off, highly structured and analytical processes as their planning tools; collecting as much data as possible and then making decisions based on this. Very few great strategies have been created this way.

Managers like to see their strategy as 'real' or 'true' to give them a sense of security, but no strategy is ever 'true.' They're all inventions and must go through a process of trial and error – one of constant refinement. Great strategies always go through numerous iterations. That's why it's important for the strategic team to stick with one facilitator over time as the strategy evolves.

Over years of facilitating strategy development with clients it's clear that developing strategy is not an event – it's an ongoing process. It's more like 'seduction' than 'deduction.' It emerges one step at a time as we solve problems and exploit various opportunities, all converging into patterns we call strategy.

"The dirty little secret of the strategy industry is that it doesn't have any theory of strategy creation. Whenever we come across a brilliant strategy, we are inclined to ask, 'Was it luck or was it foresight? Did these guys have this thing all figured out, or did they just stumble into success?'"

Gary Hamel[31]

I've found truly innovative strategies are always a bit of both luck and foresight, which can only happen in the fertile environment of experience, coincident trends, unexpected conversations, random dialogue between diverse people, and creative resolution to conflicting viewpoints and opinions. This is a lot for a manager to handle, and the easiest way to navigate this minefield of conflicting information, uncertainty and insecurity is to exclude a lot of people from the process and resort to an unemotional analytical process. Sound familiar?

Yes, deduction is a whole lot easier than seduction.

Strategising is even more than a process. In today's complex, unpredictable and ever changing world in which strategy 'emerges', strategic thinking is a capability that must be as deeply embedded in the business as customer service or total quality.

That's why strategy plays an important role in the Arrowhead and why having a clear vision and purpose is vital. Because strategy is evolving and emerging, a concept first described by Henry Mintzberg[32] in the early 1990s, it must constantly be evaluated as to how it aligns and helps facilitate the vision. Lose sight of the vision and strategy becomes no more than short-term expediency.

Imposter strategic planning

So many organisations use strategic planning not because they really believe in the process, but because it's the thing to do. The board requires it. It's public relations. *It gives a feeling of control.* It's a façade. A fad, perhaps designed to impress or give the impression all is on track – and there's no shortage of evidence to support this. Paul Nutt[33] called planning "a gesture process", citing examples of governments that hire consultants to do strategic planning to impress supporters and appease critics. How many times have we heard politicians say, "We have a plan." And a year later, when nothing has changed we hear about the next plan. Just like a broken record. How often do failing organisations announce a plan to succeed? Imposter planning serves a hidden agenda and satisfies a motivation different to its stated purpose.[34]

Focus on the strategy... not on the plan!

Think about the most successful businesses or individuals. Do they announce plan after plan? No! At most they announce a clear, simple strategy and then move step by step in that direction, and when they hit a stumbling block they adjust course, always *in alignment with the strategy*, while simultaneously checking their strategic assumptions are still correct. If not, the strategy might need to be refined.

Great leaders don't challenge results, they challenge strategic assumptions.

Interviews with leaders of 100 companies on the 2009 INC list of fastest growing private companies and recent research suggests that many successful leaders spend little time researching, analysing and planning. In fact, many companies that revere comprehensive analysis develop an incapacity for seizing opportunities.[35]

There is interdependence between strategy and operations or execution; they don't live in isolation from each other – they're joined at the hip. They operate seamlessly together in the best interests of the purpose and vision of the organisation.

In successful businesses there's a great overlap. Strategy and operations are like a great relationship. Independent Me and Independent You, coming together as Interdependent We. Not either/or but 'The Power of And.' This is the leadership challenge – to bring strategy and operations together into an interdependent win/win partnership. More on this in chapters 9 and 10.

And just as it takes ongoing conversations to build a great relationship, so to build the relationship between strategy and operations needs ongoing high quality conversations.

Leaving aside the obvious waste of resources on a collective basis – the money that could be saved if everyone stopped playing the 'imposter planning' game – it probably distorts the priorities in the business itself. Imposter planning achieves this by causing a break between the Arrowhead and Shaft. Integrity is lost because planning becomes disconnected from the strategy. It serves another 'political' or 'PR' purpose.

What differentiates genuine strategy from imposter planning is Leadership that constantly connects the Shaft with the Arrowhead. Leadership that keeps the vision and strategy constantly visible and top of mind as the organisation goes about executing. Leadership that ensures strategy is always a 'headline' and never relegated to a 'by-line', as happens in many companies.

The unfortunate reality is that imposter planning becomes a device that while used to create a semblance of control, eventually is the reason for loss of control. Planning that's not taken seriously – that's artificial instead of having substance – doesn't help managers control the organisation or the competitive environment. Imposter planning wastes time, confuses people, depletes confidence and ends up damaging organisational and management credibility.

No wonder planning is a hated process in business today. The unfortunate reality is that senior executives are usually so far removed from the Shaft of execution that they never hear the comment, "Oh no!! Here we go again. What a waste of time." I hear this all too often in my client companies.

Leadership tips: keeping strategy as a headline

> Although final strategy must be the responsibility of the most senior executives, as many people as possible should be involved in the strategic thinking process. Strategy is a team sport. Strategy succeeds in an organisation only when there is broad, varied and deep participation. How else can we achieve alignment toward the vision and build teamwork necessary to move forward? Besides, setting strategy is a creative act that can only be achieved by considering conflicting viewpoints coming from non-conformist mind-sets, resulting in what's been called 'creative abrasion.'

> The process of developing strategy must be seen as an amazing opportunity for leadership development and the process must be designed to improve strategic thinking ability. This develops the *strategic capability* I referred to earlier. We can't assume just because somebody participates in a strategy workshop that they're learning and developing themselves. Principles of adult learning need to be built into the design of the process. If you're using a facilitator ask them to explain how they'll achieve this.

> The responsibility of documenting the plan must reside in the organisation and not be delegated to outside resources. Self-documenting builds reflection, clarity and ownership, which builds commitment. When I hear, "We don't have time to write up the strategy", I'm already concerned we're creating an 'imposter' plan.

> Ensure the strategy is uncomplicated. Everyone in the organisation must easily understand it. Strategic plans that are pages long completely miss the point; length equals too detailed and complicated. Leaders can make the complicated simple.

> The plan should be communicated and communicated and communicated. Leaders communicate incessantly, simply, and creatively to ensure understanding. When Primedia Broadcasting introduced a digital element into their strategy that aligned with the way people were consuming content, initially the move was too slow. Most people nodded their head in agreement and then reverted back to what they were comfortable with, exhibiting typical denial and resistance to change. So, although most people had a foot in each camp, we divided the company into business A – the traditional analogue radio business, and business B – focused on introducing the digital strategy into the business.

Business A and business B became a strong narrative in the business. It was a powerful and yet simple way to communicate the new strategy, gain commitment, design the changes required and ensure behavioural change.

After two years the A and B were dropped because total integration of the strategy into the shaft was achieved. This was Leadership in action. Compare this to how strategy is normally communicated. A management type PowerPoint presentation, and clarity of who needs to do what by when. Who are we kidding? Ask yourself why do managers have to use PowerPoint? Usually to remind themselves of the content of their presentation. Well, if the manager can't remember it then what chance do the rest of the organisation have?

> Each department or function should then develop their own plans which clearly align with the strategy as defined in the Arrowhead. These plans must be presented to the senior executives who need to monitor for strategic alignment. In addition to indicating resources required to execute the plan, each plan should clearly indicate critical cross-functional dependencies and the support needed from other

departments to facilitate execution. Note that a strategy is not a strategy until resources are allocated to it and the required support has been negotiated and committed to.

➤ I have effectively used a simple three page or three slide approach described by Jeffrey Sampler[36], Professor of Strategy and Technology at China Europe International Business School, for departments or business units to translate the broader corporate strategy into understandable and practical unit strategies:

 ➢ Page 1: A succinct summary of the unit or departmental strategy. If you can't explain it in a few bullet points you probably don't understand it well enough.

 ➢ Page 2: The financial implications. Money required. Returns. Time frames.

 ➢ Page 3: Strategic assumptions – these are the specific elements of what you're assuming and what must happen for you to succeed, including the support you'll need from other departments.

➤ Quarterly strategy review meetings should be scheduled to review progress, check strategic assumptions and adjust plans appropriately. Leaders must ensure these meeting are not hijacked by operational issues not directly related to strategy.

➤ Performance discussions should always be framed within the context of the strategy and never in isolation from the bigger strategic picture. This again reinforces the strategy.

➤ It must become natural that problem solving and decision-making always happen in alignment with the strategy.

➤ Strategic successes should be celebrated and stories about these successes communicated.

➤ An annual strategy review should be held at the beginning of each yearly planning cycle. Teams present their last year's strategy and their execution success, which provides the starting point for the new planning period.

Doing all the above increases the probability that strategy becomes a vital part of the organisation's story, the business narrative, and people's mind-sets.

Doing this will start building a strategic capability within the whole organisation.

And that's what leaders do!

Personal strategy

Having a clear strategy is not only a fundamental requirement for success in business. It's vital for personal success as well, and every personal Arrowhead must have strategic intention in addition to purpose and vision. Strategy provides key decision triggers that focus behaviour and ensure the choices we make as we go through life always align with our purpose and vision. If we don't have a few strategic pillars, which if executed will lead to our success, we risk being pulled in conflicting directions, diluting the results we achieve. This is the main reason most individuals find themselves in a less than ideal future.

The simplest way to develop a strategy for your life is to review your purpose and vision and then answer the questions: 'How am I going to achieve this?' and 'What are the three to five most important things that will determine my success going forward?'

An illustration from my life

After I sold my business interests and started consulting I found myself with a major dilemma which would wake me up in a cold sweat at two o'clock in the morning. I had up until now created wealth in the accepted way of building and selling businesses, and although I was unhappy, I certainly achieved some financial goals. I had experienced how wealth was traditionally created. I now found myself in a position where I truly loved what I was doing but the previous strategy for wealth creation didn't apply. I would continually ask myself, "What am I doing?" I could do this until the day I retire and have no asset to sell. I might realise nil value at the end of the road.

I thought about this and came up with some strategies for this challenge. I benchmarked what other consultants had done and realised there were some options.

> I could replicate what I was doing and scale up the business by employing other consultants and so build a saleable business. I quickly realised I

would eventually slip into the role of managing a business which wasn't what made me happy.

> It was suggested I develop products to sell – videos, books etc. My first attempts at writing a book were for this reason and just didn't motivate me. I also realised I would have to build a sales organisation which would need to be managed – again the thought didn't make me happy. It was just not me.

These options might have worked for others, but they were not for me. Neither of these options aligned with my purpose – 'To be a source of inspiration and a catalyst of growth' – or with the vision I had for my personal life. I had to work out a strategy which would at all times connect my choices, decisions and behaviour to my purpose and vision, while simultaneously helping me to achieve both personal and financial goals. So I asked myself: 'What are the most important things that will determine my success going forward?' Here is an abbreviated version of my life's strategy:

> To be a premium priced consultant which would allow me to take 20% of my earnings and invest them in order to guarantee wealth creation over time, which would be roughly equivalent to my selling a medium-sized business.

> To always be at the cutting edge of business and strategy in order to deliver high value and justify a premium price. This meant constant learning and growth.

> To build an international base of clients which would expose me to current global thinking and trends.

> To achieve 70% of revenue from long standing customers who become partners. This would allow me to understand their business as an insider and help me provide solutions that really add value.

> To integrate my work seamlessly with my family life. To make the two interdependent rather than each having a space of their own.

> To have and adhere to a balanced and healthy lifestyle to ensure my ongoing physical and mental well-being.

I'm sure you can see that if I live my life according to these strategic pillars I've a great chance of living my purpose, while achieving my vision of what

I want my life to look like. What's important, however, is that this gives me direction and focus and achieves this by influencing my future choices. A good strategy will free you up to do what you need to succeed by restraining you from doing what you shouldn't be.

To illustrate:

> I can never be tempted to offer a low cost solution to a client.

> I need to find ways and means to develop an international client base.

> I read for up to two hours daily to stay up-to-date.

> I regularly attend relevant global conferences.

> If I'm going to be away from home for more than two days I always take my wife with me.

> I eat a healthy balanced diet and exercise regularly. Karate for many years, some light running, and now because of a minor back problem I walk whenever I can. I always take the stairs.

> My investments will always be financial in nature. Although my early years of being in business and in property investments created much value, I found these were exceptionally time consuming and realised that as a consultant they would definitely take my focus off my strategy of being value-adding and premium priced. So, although I have been offered several enticing business or property opportunities, as tempting as these have been, the answer has always been "no" – driven by my strategy.

These are just some of the choices I've made as a result of my strategy.

Clear. Focused. Unambiguous.

This is how I lead myself.

From the Arrowhead.

"Values give a leader courage, authenticity, integrity, conviction and persistence."

James O'Toole[37]

Chapter 8

VALUES – THE GREAT STABILISERS – THE INVISIBLE FORCE DRIVING VISIBLE RESULTS

"In all the roles I have played I have stayed committed to values-based leadership. No matter what title I've had, whether corporate executive, professor, executive partner or board member – or for that matter soccer coach, volunteer parent or Sunday school teacher, I have never lost sight of who I am and what matters to me most. By knowing myself and my values I can far more easily make decisions, no matter if I'm facing a crisis or an opportunity."

Professor Harry M Jansen Kraemer Jr.:
Northwest University Kellogg School of Business[38]

I grew up in an entrepreneurial family. My grandfather stowed away on a boat and arrived in Durban, South Africa, from Greece via Egypt at the age of 15 with no real education. He worked hard, eventually owning his own business and investing in property with every spare penny he had. He epitomised the true spirit of the immigrant entrepreneur.

He came to South Africa with nothing but a purpose – to make a better life for himself, and he did. He retired a wealthy man at the age of 34. Although he worked hard, he was a man with strong spiritual beliefs and family values. I fondly remember the regular Saturday family lunches in the garden he so loved, in the shade of a huge tree. He taught me the value of family.

I used to love sitting in his kitchen chatting with him and although at the time I didn't realise it, I was internalising consistent messages from him all the time. Work hard. Look after your money and make it work for you. Always be in control of your life. And always family, family, family. And then the unspoken messages, the loud and clear lessons that came from the exemplary way he lived his life. How he found time to balance his life, spending relaxed time in his garden with his roses. I don't think I ever saw him angry. Happy days. Positive emotions. A powerful role model and a great learning environment for a young man preparing for life. I thank him for the values and lessons he taught me.

I'll never forget when I completed school and told him I was going to university to study psychology. His comment: "My boy, I can teach you the only education you need to know. In life, it doesn't matter if you can't spell, as long as you can count." Again, that entrepreneurial self-belief that all you need in life is yourself and all things are possible.

So off I went to university to study psychology. But I'd been infused with the entrepreneurial way. My father followed in his father's footsteps, also being a successful entrepreneur with minimal education.

As with most young people, and being indoctrinated with the family entrepreneurial ethic, whilst at university I wanted to make as much money as possible, especially considering the role models I had in the family. I started a flower business at the local general hospital, getting up daily at 4am to buy flowers at the early morning flower market auctions, setting them up for the day at the hospital, and then going off to university to study.

I grew up in a family where we had a very comfortable life. I had everything I needed including sufficient pocket money to cover my daily needs, so following on my grandfather's teachings I saved all the profit from the flower business. In addition I was a drummer and played with a band, earning extra income. This too was saved, and so I completed my university studies with a sizeable bank balance.

At university I realised that although I have an incredible passion for people and human psychology, I'd developed a value and let's say a 'greed' for money, and so decided I could make more in business as an entrepreneur than as a professional. I completed my studies and took the entrepreneurial route of business.

And after 12 years and 3 successful business ventures I certainly achieved some financial goals, but something was seriously wrong.

Although I was making the money I'd set out to make I felt empty and unfulfilled. And I was physically sick all the time. Colds, flu, coughs, stomach bugs – whatever was going around, I caught. A bout of hepatitis had me laid up in bed for months and by the time I recovered I looked like a skeleton.

Towards the end of this period I enrolled in a personal development programme that totally changed my outlook and direction in life. It made me realise that in striving for my goal of making money, I'd starved and violated my values; those key priorities which were important to me. It was like being hit by lightning. A rude awakening!

So I changed careers. Using my education and business experience, together with my passion and values, I started consulting and have never been happier.

My focus on facilitating business strategy, on developing leadership, and on growing the people who turn strategy into reality, has provided THE PERFECT PLATFORM FOR ME TO LIVE OUT MY VALUES. And guess what, I still make money and in more than 30 years as a consultant I've missed only one day's work through illness. And that was through getting food poisoning. My almost twice-monthly visits to the doctor have become a once yearly check-up.

I tried to run the family relay race, picking up the baton from my father as he'd picked it up from his father. But that race was not for me. I fortunately learned the lesson early in my life – as Steve Jobs said, "You can't run someone else's race."

"Our values are the sum total of all the things we believe are good or bad, right or wrong. However, among this set of beliefs are beliefs for which we have made or would be willing to make, significant sacrifices. These beliefs I call value drivers; values we have used to drive hard choices and resolve difficult dilemmas."

David Lapin[39]

If we don't have a set of core values or priorities to live by, our lives will be pulled in so many directions, causing indecision, frustration, dissatisfaction, stress, depression and even ill health, as I experienced for so many years. Values give us the framework for living our lives, making difficult or tough decisions. They become our framework for both personal and interpersonal Leadership.

Values keep us stable in the inevitable turbulence of life. Much like with an arrow, there are crosswinds in life that tempt us, push us, pull us, and make us veer off from our goals or our course, causing us to miss our target. We end up where we didn't intend to end up, and find ourselves where we don't want to be.

That's why arrows have Fletchings (sometimes called 'vanes') at the base; they aerodynamically stabilise the arrow, keeping it on course through turbulence.

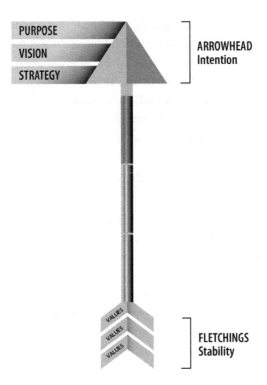

Figure 8.1: Values

Values are the Fletchings we need to keep us stable and on course as we travel life's journey.

As Fletchings are designed to keep the arrow pointed in the direction of travel by strongly damping down any tendency for the Shaft to pitch or yaw (veer off course) and keep it moving towards its intended destination, so values sit at the back of the Leadership Arrow, ensuring we don't behave in ways that clash with who we are, what's important to us, and in the process *ensuring we get these* **outcomes** *in* **a sustainable** *way... ones we can be happy with...*

It's not by chance that Fletchings are attached to the arrow at the level of behaviour.

The unpredictability and ever changing reality of life and business requires an enormous amount of flexibility of behaviour. We face unexpected challenges and hurdles on a daily, if not hourly, basis as we move toward our vision and goals. This requires constantly re-thinking plans and tactics, changing our approach, finding new and innovative options, making decisions and changing behaviour to align with all this to achieve our goals. Can you see how easy it is to choose an option and behave in ways that will certainly move us towards our goals in the short-term, but will definitely have side effect outcomes that could cause us stress and unhappiness in the longer term?

Values: a framework for living

A value is a belief or philosophy that defines who you are. A value is exactly that – something that is valuable to you. Whether we're consciously aware of them or not we all have a set of core values, acquired largely through experience but also through natural tendencies and talents we're born with. It's these values that become our framework for living; that drive our behaviour. Values indicate a strong personal preference for what's important to you, what you really care about, what kind of activities, people, work and environments you want in your life in order to be happy.

Values are powerful drivers of our lives, whether we're aware of it or not.

Values are not the soft fluff. No! Values are the hard stuff.

Values alignment

When our external world and our own behaviour align with our values, our inner world is at peace.

Aligning our goals and behaviour with purpose, vision and values infuses them with meaning, and it's this meaning that determines the amount of commitment we'll have towards a goal. Without commitment we're less likely to act in a timely fashion and are more likely to procrastinate. The more aligned our goals are with our values, the more chance of success we have. This is one of the main reasons people don't achieve their goals or live out good intentions. They don't connect their goals to their purpose and values. And how is this possible if they haven't taken the time to clarify and document their values?

"Because values play such an important role in our lives, being able to recognise, understand and articulate one's own set of values becomes critical in sound decision-making. Additionally, when an individual discovers genuine and meaningful alignment between his or her own personal values with those of his or her employer, a powerful connection is created. This connection creates numerous possibilities for both individual growth and company productivity."

Katherine W. Dean[40]

When values and behaviour clash

A clash of values or priorities is one of the major sources of inner personal dissonance, as well as a major cause of interpersonal conflict.

When our environment or behaviour contradicts our values our inner world can become incredibly stressed. The results can be experienced as inexplicable feelings of unhappiness, worry, discomfort and even depression. Note how often people cover up for a crime they committed, only to voluntarily own up many years later because they just couldn't live with themselves any longer.

Sometimes the organisation we work for has values that clash with ours, resulting in stress and unhappiness, and yet we so often neglect to understand an organisation's values before accepting a position, or an organisation will not check for value fit before hiring someone. An organisation's values will determine how it behaves – its priorities, decisions and actions. If its values clash with yours there will be ongoing conflict, unhappiness and sub-optimal performance. So often when people leave a company they say: "I just didn't fit."

How many times haven't I heard, "Sure, I've achieved my goals, but I've paid quite a price to get there." Family disintegration. Divorce or relationship breakdown. Fair-weather friends. Health problems. The rest of life slipping by…

Living a life that violates any of our core values is unsustainable and guarantees stress and unhappiness.

Values hierarchy

Values essentially reflect who we are, and as such they're relatively stable and unchanging. Contrary to what some experts might say, I believe as we move through life some of our values, based on fundamental ethical principles like 'honesty', will remain as priorities, whilst others driven by life circumstances might become new priorities. As our journey progresses values might seem like they're changing, yet they're not. Our values remain, but the hierarchy of values can change. Some cease to be priorities and others take centre-stage.

That's why it's important to constantly review values. For example, when we start our career, success, measured by advancement and recognition, might be important. But after you have a family, work-life balance might be what you value most. This doesn't mean that you don't value advancement and recognition anymore; they will always be important but suddenly they drop down the hierarchy of importance. This is why you should revisit your values, perhaps annually, especially if you're questioning your life or if it feels unbalanced or out of sync.

If I reflect on the journey of my own life I see clear phases I've travelled through, or as Gail Sheehy[41] called them in her great book of the same name, 'Passages.'

In my adult years I've travelled through some very clearly defined passages:

> Breaking away from adolescence when I went to university, during which time I met my wife.
> First career passage.
> Getting married.
> Having and bringing up children.
> Second career passage.
> Children leaving home. Empty nest.
> Recognition that life is not forever.

Each of these transitions:

➤ brought with them the roller coaster ride of change

➤ re-kindled the battle of ME vs. ME

➤ confused my thinking and created negative and uncomfortable emotions

➤ challenged me

➤ came with options on how to get through them

Some options were above the line and constructive. Some were below the line and destructive. Choices needed to be made by me, no one else, and my values both challenged and stabilised my decisions.

If I look at the evolution of my values through the phases, although many goals have changed most of my values have endured. And as they have evolved, sometimes consciously, sometimes below my awareness level, I've grown, developed, and with self-reflection, come to understand 'who I am' and what's important to me. It's amazing the focus and internal peace this brings in times of change and turbulence.

Values and coping

Nelson Mandela's 27 years in prison had purpose and therefore meaning. He did it to free a nation. He exhibited true Leadership; leading by example which reflected his purpose and values, showing who he was and what he stood for, and in the process he left a legacy. This is what great leaders do. He sat in prison because of what he believed in – his values. They gave him the strength to endure an incredibly difficult and testing situation. His values stabilised him. They gave him peace in the centre of the storm. They helped him make decisions he could live with.

To achieve anything worthwhile in life often means getting out of our comfort zone into extremely challenging and testing situations, and yes, sometimes life can be unfair. That's why it's so important to have a clear sense of direction, together with a set of core values or priorities, to stabilise us and keep us moving forward positively.

Values:

> ➤ ensure we stay true to who we are as we go about our lives
> ➤ keep us sane in times of seeming insanity
> ➤ are our stability in turbulent times
> ➤ define who we are irrespective of what is happening to us

If we have no framework for living to stabilise us and help us cope, then our daily lives can become our daily grind.

Brand values

Each of us is like a brand, and any good brand has a set of values. And just as values define a brand, our personal values define who we are. Just as a strong brand won't appeal to everyone but only to those who have similar values, so a person's individual brand won't appeal to everyone but will attract those with similar values.

When a brand tries to please everyone, brand dilution happens and it becomes wishy-washy, appealing to no one. It's the same with people, yet it's sometimes hard to accept that standing for something means everyone won't be attracted to you. Your values are a big part of defining who you are.

> *"If you don't stand for something, you will fall for anything."*
>
> Peter Marshall[42]

Values-based Leadership

When a situation arises there are two different ways we can decide on a way forward: use our experience or use our values to formulate our response. If we use our experience to make decisions, these will reflect our history in dealing with similar situations. History is always context-based, steeped in old habits and traditions, and doesn't provide the necessary adaptability to deal with new situations. But if we use our vision and values for making tough decisions, then the decisions we make will align with the future we want to create and experience. Values can be used for making tough decisions in complex situations that haven't yet been experienced. They provide a more flexible mode of decision-making.

Two different criteria for decision-making – experience and values. Yet again, it's not either/or. No! It's the 'Power of And.' Combine past experience and logical decision-making with vision and values and watch the power unfold.

Values and business

"Invisible values shape and drive visible results."

Scott Lichtenstein[43]

A leader's job is to create a vision and to inspire others to make that vision a reality. In order to get followers passionate about what they're doing, leaders have to have great energy so they can spark excitement and deliver results. While this might seem counterintuitive, a great leader sometimes needs to focus less on the numbers and more on the values of building the team and getting people to follow. According to Peter Ernest[44], CEO of Values Journey, "When a truly values based leader ensures his organisation has an ongoing process for the people to explore their personal values as well as the organisation's values, there are benefits on many levels."

In business, the real benefit of core values isn't so much those the organisation chooses, but rather how much the organisation lives them; the genuineness and passion with which they're brought to life. Values are 'valuable' only to the extent leaders are serious about them. If they're not, values can be a negative thing, because when they're not respected or implemented, mistrust and cynicism rear their ugly heads and leadership credibility dies.

Effective Leadership depends on a leader's commitment to model the values they want the workforce to adopt, and there's no shortcut to that. It requires an essential quality recognised as a vital requirement for effective Leadership: integrity.

In addition, it's impossible for the leader to be ever present in order to deal with the daily challenges followers will face and to make decisions for them.

No rule-book can predict every eventuality that followers will face. This is why managers find difficulty in delegating. Successful delegation requires empowering followers to make their own decisions. Having a clear vision and set of values provides followers with a framework within which to make effective decisions and take action timeously.

Research by Waters[45] studied the perception of numerous managers by their followers. Here are some comments regarding ex HP CEO Carly Fiorina:

> *"With Carly Fiorina there were corporate values articulated and examples of things done by Carly which were disconnected and I think that's what made a lot of people feel uncomfortable."*

> *"I was never at all sure, other than her desire to be showbiz, quite what her values were."*

Compare this comment about Mike Hurd, who followed Carly Fiorina as HP CEO:

> *"I do feel he is more mapped to the basic core values of HP than Fiorina ever was."*

> *"It was very clear what his leadership philosophy was. You knew what was important to him."*

Underlying authentic values are already there

Some values are not better than others. A value merely is, and if it's yours, it's right. As long as a value isn't immoral, illegal or harmful to others, it's legitimate. I really believe that in any culture, if you mapped out people's values you'd find great similarities, because people are people and have similar priorities in their lives. Values might manifest in different ways but the psychological need that underpins values would be similar.

My experience is that everyone has values that are important to them – even if they're not consciously aware of them – and often these values match the desired values leaders want their teams to adopt. These need to be unearthed, recognised, acknowledged, and… 'valued', in the way a leader behaves and communicates with followers.

The 'magic' resides in the way this happens. If implemented top to bottom, people tend to resist because they see values imposed as a manipulated new set of expectations – a means of control. But when they're brought about with the involvement and understanding of others, in a way that connects with their own values and aspirations, they're seen as desired standards of behaviour, with the capacity to transform 'have to' motivation into 'want to' inspiration, producing the most desired of all outcomes: engagement, performance and happiness.

A study by Lichtenstein (2005) found that executive values had a direct and significant impact on organisational performance, whereas age, tenure, functional experience, and level of education didn't. This finding indicates values as a key determinant of effective leadership.

Values are the invisible force that drives visible results.

"A framework of values or priorities is the easiest and healthiest way of leading both yourself and others. Without them, living a happy and truly successful life becomes difficult if not impossible."

Scott Lichtenstein[46]

Identifying values is not an event; it's an ongoing iterative process, as we travel through the various passages of our lives.

If you want to lead yourself and others in a way that's more rewarding, sustainable and satisfying, then:

> identify your own, your department's or organisation's values and priorities

> make them visible until they're internalised and become consciously accessible to your followers at all times

> learn to lead yourself and others through your values (see chapter 9)

> regularly re-evaluate your values and update if necessary

113

Identifying your values

Identifying your values is an ongoing introspective process. Committing yourself to the process will start making you aware of what your priorities are. Here are some suggestions to get you started:

> Google 'identifying my values' for a large number of good processes. Find one that grabs you.

> The process which has helped me most can be freely accessed on the website of a good colleague, Stef du Plessis, www.stefduplessis.com.

> Meet with an experienced and credible coach, who can help you to identify your values.

Tips for finding a suitable coach

> Use a referral service such as the International Coaching Federation. Check out their website: http://coachfederation.org.za/

> Ask for a resume together with references and do a reference check.

> Assess breadth and depth of life or business experience.

> Once you have identified a possible coach, explore their website.

> Find out what area of coaching they specialise in. Is it business, relationships, mid-life issues, etc?

> Meet for a trial session to see whether you have a rapport. Do you feel comfortable with the coach? Is this someone you can trust?

If your values don't surface immediately, keep at it and don't force them out, just document what surfaces for now. Remember it's a journey and that's what matters. Make a first draft as soon as you can, with the understanding it's exactly that – a first draft. This is vital because it gives you a launch pad for your journey. I can't stress enough how vital this first draft is.

Make them visible

Next make your values visible, even if it's only a first draft. Try using images and place them where you can easily see them. Use photos of your values to display elsewhere, such as wallpaper on your computer and phone. Images/ pictures tell a more powerful story than words do; they speak to the whole brain, both the analytical and emotional sides. This way values are internalised far quicker than if you only display them in word form (see chapter 12).

Any Leadership is based on who you are and what you stand for. It's much easier to lead through tough decisions if you have a visible and consistent framework of values as decision criteria against which to measure options. Ever been torn between two or more decisions? It's hard to decide unless you can measure the value of each decision against criteria important to you. Values give you the framework.

Next time you have a difficult decision or don't know how to handle a situation, refer to your values for the answer. They'll give you the tool to lead yourself through life.

Story

I always remember a group of American CEOs who came for a visit to South Africa with their families, spending a few days at Phinda Game Lodge in KwaZulu Natal. The visit was primarily holiday but they'd requested an educational experience as well.

One day I had them sit under some trees as family groups and asked each family to come up with a set of agreed upon values. Just to surface these took two hours of intense discussion and argument, and at the end each family prepared a visual representation of their values and presented these to the other families.

The feedback was absolutely amazing. They all commented it was probably the first time they'd experienced a discussion of this depth and meaning as individual family groups. Many family members said they now understood a lack of clarity of values was a major contributor towards conflict in the family and deteriorating relationships.

They all left with a commitment to use the values as a leadership tool in their day-to-day lives, with the understanding that the values dialogue would be ongoing, with regular review and reflection. They had begun a journey. I still get mails from some of those families thanking me for a life changing experience. I've no doubt that some families never looked at their values again. If I'm right, they lost a valuable personal and interpersonal leadership opportunity.

When you lead yourself and others from a foundation of good values, you build credibility and trust. People know what you stand for. It doesn't have to align with their values but they'll know what you stand for. It makes you a person of integrity.

Values are at the heart of Leadership.

Without values there can be no Leadership – personal or business.

PART THREE:

EXECUTION

"Only three things happen naturally in organisations: friction, confusion and misunderstanding. Everything else requires leadership."

Peter Drucker[47]

Chapter 9

LEADERSHIP IN ACTION – THE 'SMELL' OF THE PLACE

At a talk delivered to the World Economic Forum in Davos in 2004, Sumantra Goshal described organisational culture:

New context (organizational culture), some manager called it "the smell of the place", is a hard thing to describe. Let me try to describe it from my personal experience. I teach at the London Business School and live in London and have done so for several years. Before that, I lived in France and taught at INSEAD at a place called Fontainebleau. But one look at me and the sound of my voice and anyone can tell that I do not come from any of these places. My hometown is Kolkata in India. This is where my parents lived. So every year, in July, I used to go to Kolkata for almost a month. Think about it: downtown Kolkata in July. The temperature is over 100 °F with humidity of 98%. The reality was that I felt very tired during most of the vacation. Most of it I spent indoors and a lot of it simply in bed. As I said, I used to live in Fontainebleau. It's a pretty little town, 40 miles south of Paris. What makes it outstanding is that around it is the protected forest of Fontainebleau, which is one of the prettiest forests in all of Europe.

You enter the forest in spring, with a firm desire to have a very leisurely walk and there is something about the smell of the air, about the trees, that will make you want to run, jog, jump up, catch a branch, throw a stone, to do something. You will find that even though you entered the forest to have a leisurely walk, you are doing something else. Most large companies end up creating 'Downtown Kolkata in summer' inside themselves. What does 'Downtown Kolkata in summer' look like in most large companies? I relate to this in the sense of the phrase, 'the smell of the place.' Try not to intellectualise it. We intellectualise a lot in management. The reality is that you walk into a sales office, factory, head office and in the first fifteen to twenty minutes, you will get a 'smell.' You will get a smell in the quality of the hum. You will get a smell in the looks in people's eyes. You will get a smell in how they walk about. That is the smell I am talking about… What is the smell when it is a part of a large organization? Constraints! Top management is very wise, has lots of information, has good people. So, by products, by customers, by markets you create great strategies. You also work very hard – sixteen hours a day, eighteen hours a day. You take all the decisions, know exactly what needs to be done. But what does this mean for those working in the shop, in the office, sixteen levels below you? How does your hard work boil down for me, the lowly salesman? Constraints – that's what comes down to me. All the systems that top management create – human resource systems, manufacturing systems, planning systems, budgeting systems – each by itself is totally justified.

However, collectively, what does it feel for me, sixteen levels below, down on the floor? That I have to comply. All those systems hang like a black cloud over me. So I start asking myself, why does my boss exist? Not just my boss, why does the entire management infrastructure exist? As far as I am concerned, they exist for one reason and one reason alone – to control me. To ensure that I do not do the wrong thing. The job becomes a contract. The budget is a personal contract, transfer prices are contracts, relationships between colleagues and departments and divisions are all contracts. That is the environment – constraint, compliance, control, contract – that is the smell of the place. And yet what is the behaviour top management wants for me? You want me to take initiative. You want me to cooperate, voluntarily, with others around me. You want me to learn continuously and bring the benefits of that learning to my work, to my job, to the company, to its success. Where are we going to get those behaviours if this is the smell you create around me?

Execution

A few years ago I was involved in a really interesting project for a client involving spending some time in a maximum-security prison interviewing a prisoner incarcerated for 25 years for a huge cash heist in which he killed a guard. It was a fascinating experience, almost like being in a movie, to see the inner workings of a prison and to spend quality time with this individual.

What was even more fascinating was what I learned about gangs in the process. I'm not referring to the 'street gangs' we so often hear about. I was introduced to the world of highly professional gangs responsible for committing most of the major crimes in South Africa. The world of criminal syndicates – of organised crime.

The first thing I learned was that the best syndicates, or gangs, make up what's referred to as 'The Premier League', with positions in this league being understood by all members. It struck me how well-organised and professional these gangs were. Very much like a well-run organisation.

They certainly have a well-defined purpose, their reason for being. Each member has a clear understanding of their vision – their Arrowhead – which drives everything they do. They also have a clear strategy, which narrows their focus and increases their chance of success, just as any good business does. Their Arrowhead points them in the right direction and together with their strategy keeps their focus on where they should be investing energy. More importantly, the sharp Arrowhead focus also defines what opportunities they shouldn't be considering. In strategy these are called 'temptations', which can easily side-track you, taking your focus off what you should be doing, ultimately leading to failure. And failure for a gang member comes with a potentially heavy price – long prison sentences. Because of this, their execution must be perfect – and once again there are parallels to business.

The execution myth?

Goals

What is the most frequently cited requirement for success? What do most books or courses instruct you to do in order to succeed? What do most managers do to ensure execution happens and their division or department delivers?

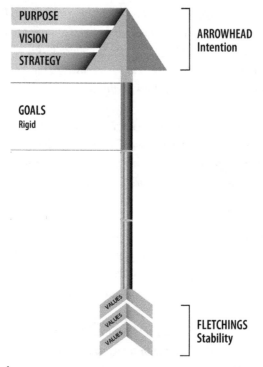

Figure 9.1: Goals

Goal setting sits at the top of the Shaft and is something widely written about in the literature. It's almost like the Holy Grail for success... a magic bullet.

Let me ask you a few questions:

How many individuals, managers and businesses have set goals to:

> start a business
> achieve a sales target
> develop a new product
> set yearly business growth targets
> change something that's not working
> lose weight
> go on a holiday
> save money
> and many more.

How many people have taken the experts' advice to write down their goals as SMART[49]?

➤ Specific

➤ Measurable

➤ Achievable

➤ Realistic

➤ Time-based

The answer would be in the hundreds of millions.

Plans

Once you have set the goal the next step in the execution process is **PLANNING.**

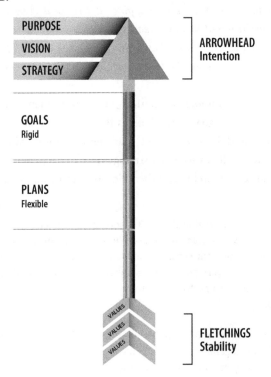

Figure 9.2: Plans

A plan spells out the steps you're going to take to get to your goal – what you need to do to achieve your goal.

➤ Sales plan: including prospecting, target market, sales call rate, etc.

➤ Savings plan for a holiday: open a savings account, deposit monthly amount etc.

➤ Weight loss plan: specific diet, etc.

➤ More complex business plans, and I've seen many impressive and detailed plans over the years.

Planning, planning, and more planning. I was really surprised at how thorough the more professional criminal gangs planned their projects. Just as detailed as the plans developed by most businesses. Whether it was for a major cash heist or a relatively minor hijacking, the planning was thorough. Don't forget, these are the most professional of gangs or syndicates. The prisoner I interviewed explained to me how he'd been shopping at the local supermarket when he spotted a well-dressed woman wearing a Rolex on her wrist and a large diamond ring on her finger. He followed her for a week to check her pattern of driving and timing to enable him to thoroughly plan the 'follow home' robbery.

Setting goals and measurable expectations, and making plans and monitoring progress against these goals and plans, is the realm of management. These tools can be found in every good manager's toolbox. Most advice on executing strategy tells us to break strategy down into doable bits, delegate these, establish accountability and then monitor performance accordingly.

I'd like to make it clear that this isn't a book about managing, nor is it my intent to minimise the role and responsibility of managing. Managing is a legitimate and important capability made up of a set of competencies that need to be part of every good manager's repertoire – one that's constantly added to, updated and perfected. Without this capability, chances of success are limited.

This is a book about Leadership. It's about the vital ingredients that can be added to the management recipe, turning good managers into great leaders; acceptable results into breakthrough performances. So as I refer to examples please understand what I describe is only *part* of the recipe. There's an assumption that a parallel, effective and appropriate, traditional management capability is in place and being utilised simultaneously.

For the sake of understanding, I've separated management and leadership as two independent capabilities. They are, however, interdependent polarities that must work together to deliver maximum performance. Like breathing in and out, absolutely vital for the body not only to survive but to thrive, so Leadership and management should happen as a pattern of ebb and flow in order for the individual or organisation to survive.

A good analogy would be a shock absorber, which facilitates the speed and safety of a motor vehicle by compressing and expanding appropriately according to the demands of the environment. In the same way, Leadership and management are both required for the speed and safety of the organisation, and both must be available at the appropriate times.

Leadership tends to expand – usually people and options, while management tends to compress – usually time and resources. The Arrowhead is about expansion while the Shaft is about compression – both need to work together to create successful performance. Again, it's not about 'either' Leadership 'or' Management. It's the 'Power of And.'

So when I quote examples, I wouldn't like you, the reader, to think, "Ha! Nick's wrong. I'm sure they just did a cost/benefit analysis", or "I'm sure their decision was based on good financial or risk management principles." Good management thinking and techniques must always be part of the recipe. The Shaft is as important a part of the arrow as the Arrowhead.

Success rate

So even with good management, whether self or organisational, what percentage of all smart goals set and elaborate plans made are ever achieved? Whenever I ask this I get answers ranging from 1% to 10%. Never more. Why is the execution success rate so poor? I've seen businesses fail despite having great strategies, smart goals, well-documented plans, and clearly defined roles and responsibilities. The critical success factor sits right at the bottom of the Shaft and furthest from the tip of the Arrowhead.

This is where the rubber hits the road. This is the step that separates the men from the boys, winners from losers, dreamers from achievers…

This is where you have to move yourself, others, your department, from the current reality (where you are now) to the goal you've set (where you want to be).

Turning a plan into reality requires action.

And action can only come from one thing – **BEHAVIOUR...** yours and others.

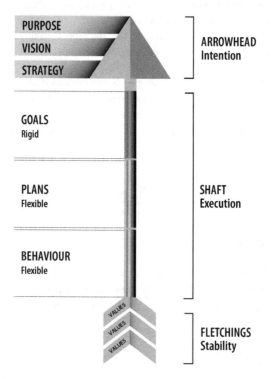

Figure 9.4: Behaviour

If you observe people at work you'll see that their behaviour as measured against a plan falls somewhere on the following scale:

ADOPTING--ADAPTING

Adopting behaviour refers to delivering exactly the behaviour required by the plan or by predetermined processes and procedures – appropriate in a predictable and well-structured environment. We're all aware of the saying,

'Everything went according to plan.' And yet how often does that happen? The reality is that the environment isn't predictable. Things constantly change, requiring us to ADAPT our behaviour in appropriate, creative and unpredictable ways. Usually the route to the goal isn't what we thought it would be.

Experience constantly shows that the critical success factor in life and business isn't the goal or the plan, although these are necessary starting and reference points. Real success always comes from having a clear long-term vision, setting a shorter term goal, fleshing out a starting point plan, and then getting into action; taking the first few steps and ADAPTING your plan and behaviour as you progress.

Come back to the incarcerated gang members. When I commented on the fact that despite all the in-depth planning they'd obviously failed, the answer was always the same: "No matter how well you plan, things don't go according to plan. The heist will evolve in an unplanned way because of unforeseen circumstances." As one gang member said to me: "It comes down to how well you can navigate yourself through the unexpected – how well you adapt. You have to think on your feet. Sometimes, sticking to the plan will kill you."

Life and business today is much the same – constant and unpredictable change. So ask yourself, how the hell can we depend on a tactical plan, which is the level of most business planning? I hear it all the time in business: "Your department isn't delivering. Give me a detailed plan on what you're going to do, with timelines and accountabilities."

The management trap

Managers are paid to get results by, with, and through other people. Their own success and job security, the very future of their career, depends on subordinates doing what they have to do. This can result in managers wanting as much predictability – as much security – as possible. Most managers want to know their subordinates have a well-documented plan with clear timelines against which they can manage and measure them. This gives the manager a feeling of control and comfort. In addition, it's great for covering the manager's own butt if things go wrong. It's ammunition the manager can later use to play the blame game.

> The Ford Pinto was a car that at one stage became notorious for its tendency in rear end collisions to leak fuel and explode into flames. More than two dozen people were killed or injured in Pinto fires. When the potentially dangerous flaw was discovered, did anyone inform Lee Iacocca, a senior executive at the time? "Hell no", said one company official. "That person would have been fired. Whenever a problem was raised that meant a delay, Lee would chomp on his cigar, look out the window and say, 'Read the product plan and objectives and get back to work.'" A focus on the execution in the Shaft without any attention to the intention in the Arrowhead. In the process, the subordinates' initiatives become stifled. Most managers spend far too much time controlling or managing – and not enough time enabling or leading.

Leaders understand, however, that:

> goals and plans don't make profits.....people do

> goals and plans don't make success.....people do

And leaders also understand that *people are not machines.*

People have hands. Yes! They do things... just as machines, and specifically robots, do. The reality is that in highly predictable environments, robots, pre-programmed with an exact plan, are replacing people. So if you're in a job where you're 'sticking to the plan', then beware. You could get replaced by technology.

People also have heads with potential to think at a highly advanced level. Some intelligent machines can think, and at a reasonably high level, but are limited to extrapolations of existing experience and information. If you're defending existing models of thinking and not thinking forward to possibilities and innovating new ways, then be aware, you could be replaced by a computer. People have hearts, emotions and feelings... no machine has!

Many managers would like to reduce their people to machines: "Just do what I tell you." Certainly this makes them more predictable and easier to manage, but it kills the heart – the seat of passion, real motivation, insight and intuition. The heart provides the fertile ground for any creativity coming from the mind to flourish in.

You can manage hands, but you can't manage heads and hearts. You can try, but all you'll achieve is suppression leading to resentment and resistance. Real success comes from engaging, rather than controlling, the hands, heads and hearts of people. Only then will they follow.

No! People don't want to be managed. It's condescending. People want to be led. Managing moves and pushes people to do what needs to be done. That's when we hear managers say: "Just stick to the plan."

Managing uses a carrot-and-stick approach.

While there's no arguing that traditional carrot-and-stick motivational approaches can produce results, they're limited by the size of the carrot and the length of the stick. No real breakthroughs or great success ever came this way.

There were no carrots or sticks involved in creating iPad for Apple, LeadSA for Primedia Broadcasting, Post-it notes for 3M, Vitality for Discovery Health.

Helping to connect people to a greater sense of purpose in what they do and how they do it will inspire them to engage at a level that no carrot-and-stick motivational techniques alone will ever do.

The LeadSA purpose and strategy of Primedia Broadcasting was vigorously debated and finally decided on by a large group of senior and middle managers. Most companies wouldn't include middle managers in the initial strategic dialogue, but CEO Terry Volkwyn understood the value that this would bring to the process. Besides which, observing how managers handle themselves in a strategic forum is a huge guide to developing their career paths and assists in succession planning.

Terry, in her wisdom and despite her impatience, allowed the original LeadSA debate to go on for two full days. She understood the importance of thorough understanding and buy in. In 17 years of facilitating strategy for Terry, never once did we use an agenda. The only scheduled items were starting and finishing times, and breaks. And as with the LeadSA debate, if one day was not enough, we continued on another day. This was pure leadership in action. The average number of days allocated to strategy development yearly at Primedia Broadcasting was 10. Perhaps that's why she was named 'Boss of the Year' and subsequently 'Woman of the Decade in Media'!

Most successful strategies are created, refined, and executed by people at all levels of the organisation – people who put in extra thought, extra commitment, extra effort and extra creativity, over and above what's required by any job description, tactical plan or management decree.

Breakthrough results are created by people… and Leadership.

➤ Leadership that 'expands.'

➤ Leadership that attracts and pulls.

➤ Leadership that gets people to *want to do* whatever is required to get things done to achieve success.

➤ Leadership that frees and enables people to use their heads and hearts to choose the right behaviour at the right time in order to achieve the outcome required.

➤ *Leadership that empowers and encourages people to lead themselves.*

For people to lead themselves they need to know where they're going. If they don't, they act in ways that are inappropriate within the context of the bigger picture. Empowerment means being free to set a path, choosing how to get there from numerous options, making decisions, and solving problems. How is this possible without understanding the bigger picture; without being connected to the Arrowhead?

The polarities dilemma

"Polarities are interdependent pairs that support a common purpose and one another. They are energy systems in which we live and work."

Dr Barry Johnson – Polarity Partnerships[50]

Great leadership and breakthrough execution comes from infusing the execution in the Shaft with the single-minded purpose, vision and strategy of the Arrowhead. The Shaft is what gives the Arrow impetus. Here we have two seeming polarities which can tear each other apart or can work as legitimate partners in the journey towards success. It's not Either/Or. No! It's the 'Power of And.'

&

Success in the end comes from **Effective Leadership** that provides meaning and direction AND **Efficient Management** that ensures impetus and agility. The Arrowhead *and* the Shaft. The following represents four possible outcomes that can result from these two elements.

1. STRONG ARROWHEAD + STRONG SHAFT = SUCCESS

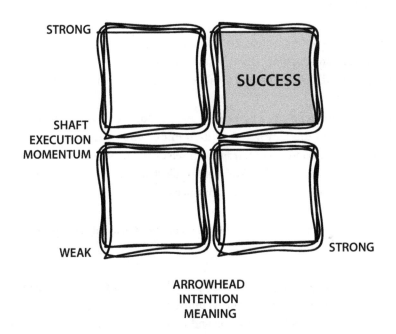

Figure 9.6: STRONG ARROWHEAD + STRONG SHAFT = SUCCESS

This is exemplified by the companies referred to in earlier chapters, like Apple, Google, Primedia Broadcasting, RE/MAX, TOMS Shoes and many more.

All these companies have effective Leadership but they also have efficient management. How often do we read biographies of great leaders, are inspired by their sense of purpose and vision (expansion), and yet are sometimes shocked and even disappointed when we see how tough they can be in dealing with people who don't execute (compression).

Having worked with so many successful business owners, CEOs, managers and sportspeople, there are certain descriptors that always seem to be related to success. Let me list the most common:

Committed. Never give up. Passionate. Resilient. Relentless. Bold. Hard on what needs to be done. Driven. Determined. Assertive. Aggressive. Impatient. Perfection. Stretch. More. The best. Win. Action. Intolerant. Tough. Find a way. Solutions.

I think of Steve Jobs of Apple; Liz Kobilski of Rich products; Terry Volkwyn of Primedia Broadcasting; Duncan Lewis of Pack n Stack; Helen Zille of the Democratic Alliance and many, many more. Add your own examples.

Yes! Successful people can be hard on others, but they are even harder on themselves, and this clearly reveals itself in execution – in the Shaft of the Arrow. They demand the best from themselves and they demand the best of others. I have never seen breakthrough results being achieved with anything less than this level of drive and commitment.

The problem is that this can either break people and disengage them, or build people and turn them into followers.

The determining factor is Leadership, and Leadership can only happen when this intense drive to execute is infused with the passion coming from common purpose and shared vision and values. The execution – in the Shaft of the Arrow – must at all times be based on the legitimate intention of the Arrowhead. This adds meaning to tough demands and legitimises the leader's relentless pursuit for excellence in execution, infusing his behaviour with integrity and credibility – two qualities without which leadership can never happen.

Leaders like Steve Jobs exhibit behaviour that most would regard as unacceptable and unsustainable. And yet they seemingly 'get away with it.' The difference lies in the Arrowhead. Their purpose and vision are clear, and they are constantly and effectively communicated to all stakeholders. They are hard on behaviour *because of what they're trying to achieve – the Arrowhead.* The behaviour is only problematic because it interferes with where they are going and that's not acceptable. In fact if their vision can't be your vision as well, then you shouldn't be there.

To use Jim Collins' (2001) analogy: "You should know where this bus is going and then you're either on the bus or off the bus." Great leaders will sometimes rant and rave because you're interfering with the direction and speed of the Arrowhead, rather than discipline your behaviour in isolation from the Arrowhead.

Leaders connect non-performance in the Shaft to the intention of the Arrowhead and then deal with it from there.

Herein lies the power of the Arrowhead. It raises the awareness and reason for being in the Shaft to above the individual job description level; above the departmental goal driven level; and right into the level of purpose, vision and strategy. Leaders make it clear why we're here, what we're trying to achieve and how we're going to get there, and they'll manage non-performance within this context. So when they discipline, yes, they refer to the unacceptable performance, but they connect it and its consequences to the Arrowhead.

Note the difference between the following statements:

"Your overloading that client with stock was unacceptable."

vs.

"Your overloading that client with stock was unacceptable! It doesn't align with our strategy of building win/win partnerships with our clients. It also clashes with our value of 'mutual respect.' It definitely isn't going to help us achieve our vision of 'building a sustainable business we can all be proud of."

The first statement is a typical management response to non-performance and deals with the issue in the limited context of the offending behaviour, the job description, and the Shaft. The stories in both the manager's and follower's head could be different. The manager's story is about not wanting the subordinate to overstock clients. The subordinate's story could be about achieving his sales target and getting his bonus. Two different stories, two different agendas. When you try to manage people this way it can degenerate into a you vs. me situation. "You don't understand" or "You're on my case" or "You just don't like me."

The second statement raises the issue to a higher non-negotiable level; the definitive common purpose, vision, strategy and values of the organisation. Together these result in the organisation's single-minded intention – it's non-negotiable 'Formula for Success.' The Arrowhead embodies the fundamental principles that determine what's acceptable and what's not acceptable as we move forward. Every individual in the organisation must be aware of and align their behaviour with these non-negotiables.

Align with the Arrowhead or get off the Shaft

The Arrowhead is never up for debate – you either align or 'get off the Shaft.' Non-alignment should be handled in a way that sends a clear message to the organisation. Leaders must walk the talk. If they say something is non-negotiable, their behaviour should clearly reflect it. This is how followers internalise the Arrowhead. This is how leaders get credibility. This is why people follow leaders. This is why Leadership isn't a 'soft' issue as some hard core traditional managers see it. I repeat – Leadership is not soft fluff. In fact, it's about the hard stuff.

2.   STRONG ARROWHEAD + weak shaft = unachieved vision

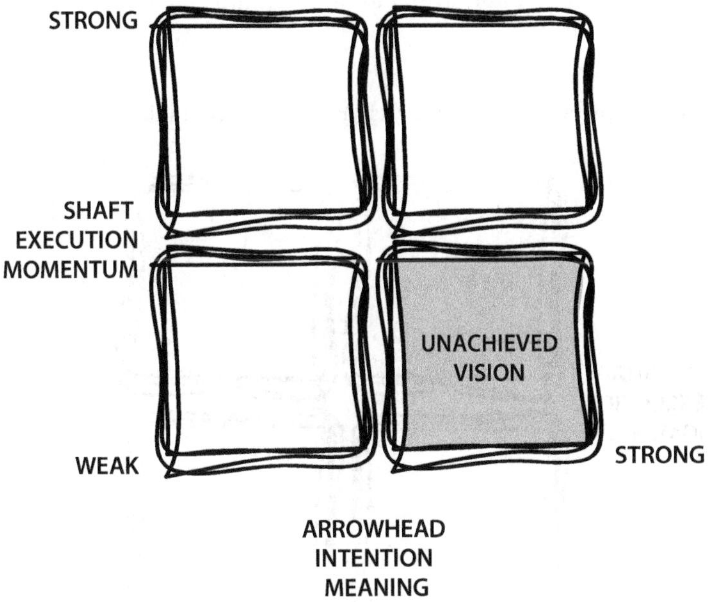

Figure 9.7: STRONG ARROWHEAD + weak shaft = unachieved vision

Too much Arrowhead and not enough Shaft will have us pointing in the right direction but going nowhere.

This situation is unfortunately so often the norm. People dream of the life they'd like to have but never get there. Their vision remains unfulfilled. Comments like, "I'll do it tomorrow", "I'll start when..." or "As soon as I have the budget", are typical in this situation. Another example of the tramp in full flight. There's a lack of urgency and discipline to execute, leading to disappointment and living below the line, feeling like a victim of circumstances and playing the blame game.

Both people and businesses find themselves here when they have a clear vision of the future, but cannot let go of old approaches or ways of doing things. An inability to change behaviour is one of the major reasons for unachieved visions or dreams.

Too much wanting and not enough doing of the right things! Too much Leading and not enough managing.

If this sounds like you then activate your Shaft by asking yourself, "What are the first three steps I must take in to move towards my vision or dream?" Take them!

3.   weak arrowhead + STRONG SHAFT = on a treadmill

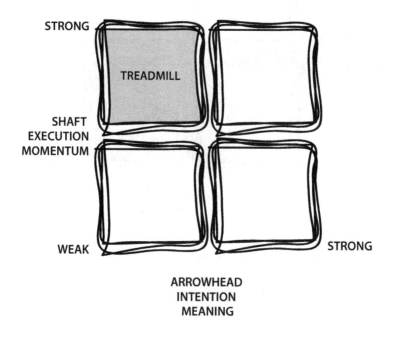

Figure 9.8: weak arrowhead + STRONG SHAFT = on a treadmill

This is the most frequent scenario I've seen in business and life. Setting high shorter-term targets and standards; working incredibly hard to achieve them; feelings of pressure, stress and frustration; leading to burnout and comments like "Why am I so unhappy?", or "I don't seem to be able to switch off?" Always striving, always pushing harder for that elusive thing called success and although achieving results, never feeling a sense of joy in what you're doing or achieving. Remember the group from Orlando? How many people look forward to retirement simply to escape the treadmill of imposter success?

This story is a great example of the SHAFT operating with no or minimal Arrowhead.

My diary with clients, especially those on other continents, is usually booked well in advance, as was this trip. It's the beginning of December 2014 and I have a few days consulting in the USA after which my wife and I are on vacation. Our flights were booked well in advance and I ensured we'd been pre-seated together.

When I did an on-line check-in 24 hours before flight time I discovered my confirmed pre-seating had been changed and my wife and I were not seated together. After years of flying I have the highest loyalty status at South African Airways and so I phoned their Platinum Desk to be told my originally booked seats had been allocated to someone else. It took four hours of the agents blaming, pointing fingers and excuses to find two seats next to each other – clearly operating 100% from the Shaft and from below the line. At one stage they claimed I hadn't confirmed pre-seating, so I forwarded their email confirmation. In the meantime I'd studied the available seats on-line and suggested a solution. The operator said she didn't have the authority to make the adjustment, so I asked to speak to a supervisor who wasn't available.

On my suggestion, the operator said she'd escalate the issue and call me back. During the next three hours I called her numerous times only to be told she wasn't available and would call me back. When I eventually pinned her down she said she wanted to wait for the next flight controller to come on duty because: "This controller will understand and sort out the problem", which is what happened.

This controller operated from a strategy context rather than merely from an operational context. Now I realise we can't have everybody being empowered to adjust seating on flights, but we can create an understanding encouraging people to place the strategy as a priority, motivating them to stay above the line, proactively working within operational rules and procedures to find a win/ win solution. The agent could have proactively led the process to the eventual solution rather than have me lead it. Expansive Leadership within compressed management processes and procedures. The 'Power of And.'

This is the background to those situations where a turnaround CEO comes into a business with one purpose: 'Make the business profitable.' The focus is totally on the Shaft and short-term metrics. These people are generally ruthless and demanding and once they've turned the business around they leave with all the glory – leaving a non-sustainable situation for the next CEO to deal with. Too much Shaft and no Arrowhead!

When winning becomes the purpose

In my 30 years of consulting something I've noticed is the competitive attitude of people who make it to the top. They like to win. Even more so, they don't feel satisfied unless they do win. And when they win, they like others to know they've won. The need for winning is generally impatient. It can't wait five years. Short-term results feed it and satisfy it. A strong competitive spirit and need for winning are a great strength to have and a definite requirement for execution and success in any arena of life, but unbridled competitiveness can lead to behaviour which might help us succeed and feed our need in the short-term, but can cause problems in the long-term.

Lance Armstrong is a devastating example of this.

Unmanaged competitiveness can disconnect the Shaft from the Arrowhead.

4.   weak arrowhead + weak shaft = surviving

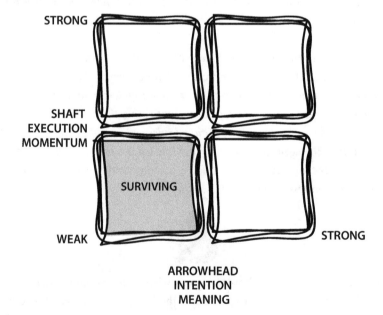

Figure 9.10: weak arrowhead + weak shaft = surviving

Same s**t, different day

Of course this worst-case scenario is so often the reality for so many businesses and individuals.

➤ Weak Arrowhead and inefficient Shaft.

➤ Living day by day. Forging on, 9 to 5.

➤ Surviving but definitely not thriving.

➤ Making a living but not making a life.

This is the realm of total disengagement and entitlement; not going anywhere and not being prepared to put in any effort.

The stabilising role of values

It's not sufficient to have both a strong Arrowhead and a strong Shaft. Without the Fletchings, environmental turbulence can so easily nudge or even knock the arrow off its path. In the same way, short-term demands and daily pressures can impact on our lives and our businesses. Values provide us with the wherewithal to navigate through this turbulence, keeping us on track in a balanced way. When we violate our values, we veer off course.

An arrow needs to have an Arrowhead, a Shaft, and Fletchings. Only then is perfect flight possible.

And note how the values in the Fletchings are directly connected to the behaviour at the bottom of the Shaft. At all times, behaviour should be modeled on our values. More often than not, when we get ourselves into trouble and veer off course in our lives it is because we have violated a value. As Stephen Covey said, "It's so hard to talk yourself out of a problem you have behaved yourself into."

Values inform appropriate and inappropriate behaviour, ensuring stability and sustainability in our businesses and our lives.

Balance

So where does the balance between the Arrowhead, the Shaft and the Fletchings lie? Remember the science of an arrow from chapter 4? It gives us the answer. You will recall that arrows have what is called an FOC (forward of centre) score or rating. This refers to the point at which you can balance the arrow on your finger. The best arrows have a FOC point on the upper end of the Shaft near to the point where the Shaft joins the Arrowhead. To achieve the ideal balance between direction and impetus the best arrows have 60% of their weight in the Arrowhead and 40% of their weight in the Shaft. Most importantly, the Arrowhead and the Shaft are one. They're joined. Where they go, they go together.

*Similarly, in a life or a business, the vision and strategy should **permanently** be joined to behaviour and the **weighting** should be **60% Arrowhead** and **40% Shaft**.*

Permanently joined doesn't mean we have a strategy workshop, agree on the strategy at a senior level and then forget about it while we attack our Shaft short-term targets to ensure results. No! Permanently joined means exactly that. Joined at the hip! Where one goes, the other goes. 24/7. There's a huge difference.

The implication of the **60/40 balance** is that we should keep our vision and strategy at the forefront of our minds as we act; it's a reference point for everything we do. Implementation should always align with the context of our Arrowhead. Any choices, decisions and behaviours should be guided and informed by our vision and strategy.

Before the Tylenol crisis in 1982, when a malevolent person replaced Extra Strength Tylenol capsules with cyanide laced capsules, Tylenol was responsible for 33% of Johnson and Johnson's year-to-year profit growth and accounted for a 37% market share. Had Tylenol been a corporate entity unto itself, profits would have probably placed it in the top half of the Fortune 500.

This is a great example of managing a crisis in the Shaft. Although there was little chance of finding more cyanide-laced capsules and J&J could have simply removed all capsules from the particular store or even from all stores in Chicago, limiting their financial damage in the short-term, they decided to pull the product from all stores in the USA. This, according to various communications and interviews, was based on their core credo: "We believe that our first responsibility is to the doctors, nurses and patients, to mothers and fathers and all others who use our products and services." A courageous leadership decision informed by the Arrowhead more than the practical implications in the Shaft. The result: although they lost millions in the short-term, J&J leadership sent a clear message about what they stand for. J&J eventually completely recovered its market share and the Tylenol brand name is one of the most trusted over-the-counter consumer products in America.

This is how leaders build credibility. Their Arrowhead is clear, the Fletchings monitor behaviour, and they walk the talk – they model the way. The link to the Arrowhead is visible for all to see. Sure, I know many executives do make decisions based on their own or the organisation's Arrowhead, but they lose a wonderful leadership opportunity by not making it visible.

The mistake some managers make is thinking everyone needs to be aware only of the final decision and not how the decision was made. *The Arrowhead and values should provide important non-negotiable decision-making triggers or criteria which are clearly communicated and understood.* This is how leaders create alignment between the Arrowhead and people's behaviour in the Shaft.

The Arrowhead should not be seen as a decorative adornment, but rather as a set of decision-making touchstones and reference points that can be used by everyone in the organisation.

Arrowhead erosion

When shorter-term incentive driven goals and plans become valued over and above the Arrowhead, we get what I call "Arrowhead erosion." Many managers are guilty of rewarding only results, which are in the Shaft, rather than high quality decisions taking both the Arrowhead and the Shaft into consideration... a potential recipe for disaster over the long-term.

➢ At the heart of the 2008 universal financial crisis was President Bill Clinton's desire to increase home ownership during his Presidency and the decisions he made between 1993 and 2001 to achieve this. These decisions led to unintended consequences. Numerous commentators suggested that President Bill Clinton's name should be added to a long list of people who deserve a share of the blame for the housing bubble and bust. He seemed to have gone to ridiculous lengths to increase the national homeownership rate. This promoted paper-thin down payments and pushed for lenders to give mortgage loans to first-time buyers with shaky financing and incomes. It's clear that the erosion of lending standards pushed prices up by increasing demand, and later led to waves of default by people who should never have bought a home in the first place.

➤ South Africa's Arrowhead describes the very meaningful purpose and vision of a thriving country of equal opportunity for all people; an important and valid pillar of the strategy to achieve sustainable Black Economic Empowerment. In the Shaft we have the goals and plans to measure this, and remember that in relation to the Arrowhead, the BEE targets are only metrics and not the strategy itself. Metrics in the Shaft should only exist within the context of the Arrowhead. When the metrics become the purpose, disaster looms. The goals and metrics are achieved, and the real price of achievement is the erosion of South Africa's Arrowhead and then longer term sustainability of the country.

The price South Africa is paying by focusing only on BEE targets is high. Emigration of vital talent; inexperienced people in critical roles; cost of available talent rapidly increasing; cost of living rising; increasing income gap between wealthy and poor; a wealthy country's resources stretched to the limit; services not being delivered… the list goes on and on.

Almost daily I notice the inherently unsustainable decisions being made in the quest to achieve BEE targets. Please note that I'm not suggesting that the purpose, vision and strategy of BEE are incorrect – I really believe they're essential. What BEE needs is Leadership to ensure we keep the real meaning and purpose of BEE top of mind as we execute, and confront possible de-stabilising side effects, while facilitating a new sustainable approach for achieving the purpose and delivering on the strategy. After all, the targets are not the purpose. The targets are in the Shaft. The targets are only a result. A thriving economy and accelerated empowerment together make the vision. It's the 'Power of And', not one at the expense of the other. Having BEE targets that have become disconnected from the real purpose of empowerment is creating 'the smell of the country.'

The message is clear.

The trap we fall into is thinking that Execution (Shaft) = Success. Wrong.

Intention (Arrowhead) + Execution (Shaft) + Values (Fletchings) = Success.

Intention comes from Purpose, Vision and Strategy.

Execution comes from Goals, Plans and Behaviour.

Stability and sustainability come from values.

Boost the immune system

The Arrowhead and the Fletchings are the immune system of the organisation. They keep the organisation healthy and deal effectively with any viruses or bacteria that enter at the Shaft level. Effective leaders use the Purpose, Vision, Strategy and Values to keep the immune system as strong as possible.

The ideal manager should play a doctor's role. Just as a doctor knows and monitors strategic vital signs of health, such as blood pressure, heart rate, cholesterol levels, etc., so the manager should know and monitor the key strategic metrics responsible for his business or his department's health. These range from higher-level organisational metrics such as turnover, profit, margin or whatever the business measures its health against, to KPIs at individual job level. And just as a good doctor will give only enough medication to support the body's effective immune system, always being aware of and monitoring the possible side effects of treatment, so the wise manager will intervene only enough to support and enable the followers' ability to perform. This is empowerment. Unfortunately some doctors are guilty of over-medication, achieving a quick and remarkable resolution of present symptoms only to leave side effects that cause future problems. Many managers are guilty of over managing or controlling when performance isn't happening, unaware of the side effects of what they do. This causes new problems which then have to be managed and controlled. 'The smell of the place…'

In the same way patients can become addicted to medication, so subordinates learn to depend on managers' intervention when initiative needs to be taken.

The major retailer I referred to in an earlier chapter created exactly this problem. In order to give head office management a sense of control over dropping standards, store managers had so many management checklists to fill in and so much reporting to do they started neglecting fundamental strategic success factors like:

➤ 'eyeballing' the store for appearance

➤ connecting with staff as they carried out their duties in order to build engagement

➤ communicating with customers to understand their requirements

A comparison group of franchisee owner-managers relegated the required head office checklists and daily reports to a low priority level, which often caused conflict between them and the franchisor head office, yet the performance and standards of their stores consistently outperformed the company-owned stores. The difference was that in the franchise stores the Arrowhead was given priority over the Shaft, and not vice versa.

It's said that at least 50% of disease is iatrogenic in origin, coming from two Greek words, 'Iatros', meaning 'doctor', and 'Genic', meaning 'beginning.' It's caused by treatment given for a previous illness. The treatment has side effects which become new problems, as when an anti-inflammatory causes bleeding in the stomach. This needs a proton pump inhibitor to reduce stomach acidity, and so the process goes. There's a fine balance between supportive treatment and over medication. To achieve this balance a good doctor needs:

➤ a total understanding of the human body

➤ to understand and accept the power of the body's immune system to keep it healthy

➤ an ability to diagnose a situation correctly, both proactively and reactively

➤ a toolbox of appropriate treatments

➤ a full awareness of and sensitivity to the possible side effects of the treatment

➤ the judgement to intervene as little as possible while encouraging the patient to adjust their lifestyle as a first priority

➤ the credibility and bedside manner that motivates the patient to do what is required

(Bear in mind that there certainly are those emergencies where dramatic short-term intervention might be required which is deemed to be an absolute priority.)

Similarly, a manager should:

> - have an understanding of the nature of people

> - know that culture (the smell of the place) is the organisation's immune system and is built through the Arrowhead and the values

> - understand that if empowered, most people want to do the right thing and want to succeed

> - know how to diagnose a situation correctly

> - have a toolbox of appropriate approaches for dealing with non-performance (treatment)

> - have an awareness and be sensitive to the possible side effects of any treatment for non-performance

> - have the judgement to intervene (manage) as little as possible while encouraging the person to adjust their own workstyle where necessary (lead)

> - have an interpersonal style and behave in ways that build credibility and gain followers

Keeping the Arrowhead vital

Leaders keep the immune system of the organisation vital by keeping the Arrowhead vital, yet Arrowhead fatigue is a common organisational affliction that can surface at any time, from the finalisation of the vision and development of the strategy through to strategic planning and the execution in the Shaft. You know your company is a victim when the committees formed to "work out the details" of the strategy meet less frequently and with less enthusiasm. Or when planning becomes, once again, a numbers exercise with hardly a mention of the strategy. Or when you listen to discussions taking place and find out not much is being said about strategy.

If the leader's aim is to sustain strategy over the long haul then strategy must be continuously infused into the Shaft. Strategy must become part of the organisation's culture and the performance evaluation of managers and individuals. You know you're successful when strategy becomes part of what everyone is doing; when everybody knows what this is and why it's so, and commits to achieving the strategy in every decision made, every action taken.

"Creating a strategic capability throughout the whole organization is possibly the last real competitive edge."

Jeffrey Sampler – Adjunct Professor of Strategy and Technology: China Europe International Business School[51]

When Chet Marks of the Dow Chemical Company said: "Today, having a common reference point is the only sustainable way to carry a business forward", he was referring to a common Arrowhead.

Sharing the same reference point doesn't mean everybody must march to the same drumbeat; it ensures we're all marching in the same direction yet leaves plenty of room for creativity and self-expression. It's what real empowerment is about. Yes, in a world of constant change and unpredictability, where resilience and adaptation are needed to keep organisations relevant and competitive, strategic thinking must be infused into the whole organisation.

So how do you empower the Shaft with the focus and energy created by the Arrowhead? How do you keep the Arrowhead vital?

> - Ensure you allocate the required time, not the least time possible, to allow for adequate strategic dialogue.

> - Organisational Purpose, Vision and Values must be reviewed annually and be top of mind at any strategic session.

> - The leader must model the way for the 'expansion' to happen, playing a strong listening role to create an environment that legitimises people and encourages contribution and challenge without fear of being embarrassed. In a strategy discussion, anything goes. Don't kill the messenger.

➤ Implementing strategy is more than a roadshow with 'death by PowerPoint' presentations. It must be achieved through tried and tested change management principles and communication that sticks. The process must move people out of 'denial' and deal with their 'resistance', while 'enabling' them to execute their new responsibilities in line with the strategy. This takes time, which is what managers claim not to have enough of. **Leaders know different**. To them this is a priority, so they make the time.

➤ Remember the Arrowhead represents a story and communicating effectively can only be achieved through good storytelling. (Chapter 12 will deal with this in more detail.)

➤ Metrics and incentives need to be reviewed to ensure they will drive only Arrowhead-aligned behaviour and won't encourage actions taking the arrow off course. Remember incentives are a solution, like medicine, that can have side effects. Incentives often lead to problematic outcomes. The solution? More medicine is the usual approach. It also helps to make managers feel like they have everything under control. Oh yes, and helps to 'cover butt.'

➤ Review all management systems, reporting processes and routine procedures to make sure they align with the Arrowhead. Trim these to the bare minimum to free up people to do what really adds value. A good doctor will give you the smallest dose of medication needed. Unfortunately organisations adopt new strategies and then stick to old mechanisms for managing the business or department. This is like adding one remedy on top of another, each with its own side effects. Remember that more often than not, 'less is more.' Ask managers to review the Arrowhead and then present three things their department will no longer do. Never forget strategy is not only about creating a focus on what to do – it also tells us what not to do.

➤ The Arrowhead should be part of the curriculum for any training, whether internal or outsourced. Training outcomes must be directly linked to the organisation's Arrowhead, and not only as a course opener, but through ongoing reference at all stages of the process. Trainees should clearly understand how the new competencies add value to the Arrowhead. Leaders use every opportunity for reinforcing the message and the training room is such an opportunity. Unfortunately, it's usually wasted.

> Performance management, whether involving either positive or negative feedback, should always be linked to the Arrowhead. Another great opportunity for Arrowhead reinforcement.

> The Arrowhead and Fletchings should form an important part of the recruitment assessment process. The biggest reason why some people don't perform is because they just don't fit. They had all the qualifications and competencies for the job, but their personal purpose, vision and values didn't align with the organisation's. Shaft competencies are a lot easier to teach than Arrowhead qualities.

> Ample opportunity must be found to tell Arrowhead-related stories and to celebrate success. I encourage clients to communicate and document all such stories. Some even put these into book form. These stories become the legends that communicate very clearly who we are, what we stand for, how we should behave and how we are going to succeed. These stories keep our Arrowhead vital.

Chapter 10

THE FLIGHT PATH FROM
'ME' TO 'WE'

*You cannot do it without the support of other people
and, you are not entitled to it. You have to earn it.*

As our braai guests in chapter 3 unanimously agreed:

➤ "Don't hang onto your hurdles"..........Yes

➤ "If it's going to be, it's up to me"........Yes

But they all unanimously agreed that "You can't do it without the support of other people", and they repeated over and over again, "You're not entitled to that support, you have to earn it."

The statement "I don't need anyone in my life" is the epitome of denial; usually the line taken by people who can't build relationships and partnerships with others.

Research consistently shows that healthy and supportive relationships can reduce stress, improve your general sense of well-being, and be catalysts for above average performance.[52]

The reality

> **We can't fly without the support of other people.**

> We don't live our lives in isolation from others. Isolation is a word used in association with punishment.

> We're connected physically, emotionally and psychologically with other people. There are always other people in our lives. The 'Story of my Life' has many actors. Some play leading roles, others supporting roles and then there are many extras, all contributing in a minor way to my vision. Anyone who believes they can have a successful life by doing it alone, in isolation, is in denial and delusional. No successful life can exist without other people.

> The state of the relationship between two or more people will determine the support that is willingly given or the extent to which a human being will willingly follow someone else. Without this support leadership isn't possible.

> Positive relationships help keep our thoughts focused and they nourish us emotionally. They bring out the best in us, help us to make meaningful progress and facilitate our success. They enable us.

> Negative relationships are toxic; they hijack our thinking, sabotage our emotions and make it difficult for us to act. They drain us and slow down our lives, our progress and our success.

Reflection

Think of a positive relationship in your life, either personal or at work. How does this relationship impact on your thoughts, feelings and behaviour? How does it impact your motivation and energy levels?

Now, think of a negative relationship. What effect does this relationship have on your thoughts, feelings and behaviour? How does it impact your motivation and energy levels?

Leadership as a partnership

"Problems can become opportunities when the right people come together."

Robert South[53]

Life is rich with diversity and in today's interdependent world, driven by weakening of boundaries and easy global connectedness, it's either/or thinking that leads to so many of the problems we're confronted with in life, relationships and business. Real value and growth can only be created when two or more diverse worlds and perspectives come together.

It's my belief that in business today, where strategies are easily duplicated, the ability to build partnerships that co-create value is one of the last sustainable competitive edges that exist. And once you've achieved it, it's hard to duplicate.

Similarly, in relationships it's the value we create together that makes the relationship sustainable in a world full of challenges.

Let's have a look at the partnership journey in order to understand how supportive, value-building partnerships are created.

The partnership journey

The following relationship stages are adapted from the work of Australian corporate psychologist, Greg Nathan, also Founder of the Franchise Relationships Institute. Greg Nathan has researched the emotions and expectations people have of each other when they are in interdependent business relationships and mapped these into a model he calls "The Franchise E-Factor"[54].

Successful win/win partnerships and relationships often follow a predictable path.

In the sketches that follow:

Above the line = Happiness
Below the line = Unhappiness

Please note that the model that follows has a number of stages, which do not all necessarily have to flow as described. Some stages could be skipped and it's also possible to regress to an earlier stage.

Most relationships begin their journey in the stage of GLEE.

CO-CREATING VALUE: THE PARTNERSHIP JOURNEY

Figure 10.1: GLEE

This is the romance stage – a stage of high expectation and happiness. I'm excited by the potential a relationship with you presents. Wow! You and I. What a team we could make. Together we could really fly to new heights.

In this stage the communication flows easily and the relationship hums with possibilities. 'Influence' and 'partnership' are two words that epitomise this phase of the relationship journey. Communication flows. Both sides have value and both sides are considered and valued. The relationship has great promise.

The next phase of the journey is FEE.

CO-CREATING VALUE: THE PARTNERSHIP JOURNEY

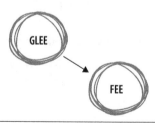

Figure 10.2: FEE

Here my level of happiness drops somewhat. I begin to realise that if I want an ongoing relationship with you there's a price to pay. I can't always have things my way. There are now two of us to consider. Two sets of needs. Two ways of doing things. Dissatisfaction grows.

Eventually my level of dissatisfaction pushes me under the happiness/unhappiness threshold into stage three, ME.

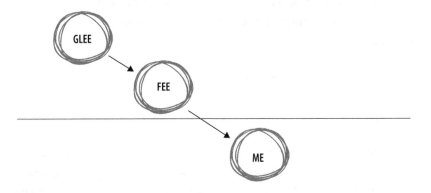

CO-CREATING VALUE: THE PARTNERSHIP JOURNEY

Figure 10.3: ME

This is a self-focused area. ME; my ego (my tramp) now starts telling me that I'm paying too much. This relationship is costing me. I start measuring what I'm giving and what I'm getting back in return. I do a cost-benefit analysis and am unhappy that I'm giving more than I'm getting.

I start asking questions: "Is this my life?" "Is this what it's all about?" In marriage, this phase used to be called the seven-year itch. Experts say it's now the eleven-year itch. This is the time when I'm most likely to evaluate my situation and possibly look for greener pastures. In the ME phase I'm susceptible to a new relationship because that takes me right back into the GLEE phase with its novelty, excitement and promise. Like an addict I need a shot in the arm to give me a renewed kick, not realising any new relationship will eventually move through the FEE stage and into the ME stage with all its resentments.

In business we hear comments like, "I'm the one carrying the load here. She gets paid the same as me but leaves most of the work to me. This is unfair." Resentment rears its ugly head. It's in this stage that people think about putting out their CVs.

We start fighting more than normal. Support for each other reduces to what is absolutely necessary and no more. We attack each other or we just become passive and withdraw. We have now become two MEs, relating at tramp to tramp level. There is my tramp and your tramp, both in high protective mode. I've now really had enough of the seeming injustice. I now feel like a victim and am below the line. Pointing fingers and blaming are characteristic of this phase.

Two egos looking after their own interests.

Managers and workers protecting their own agendas.

In this phase, for the sake of peace, the partnership can become a contractual relationship – I'll do what I'm supposed to do, you do what you're supposed to do. It's clear no real value can be created like this. I often see this value limiting situation – both in personal relationships and in business.

It's sad so many people resign themselves to living in this phase. They accept this as their lot in life. The relationship continues, if only at a level of practicality. Roles could be defined and as long as individuals behave themselves and deliver according to role expectations, life carries on. No energy. No real value other than convenience.

At this point, however, the decision to FLEE this partnership becomes a distinct possibility.

CO-CREATING VALUE: THE PARTNERSHIP JOURNEY

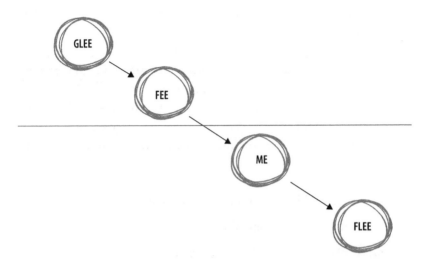

Figure 10.4: FLEE

FLEE, although an easy choice after ME, is not the only option. As always happens, there's another choice I'm free to make. Instead of moving to FLEE, I might SEE the positive that already exists and the potential value that could still be created by two people in a true partnership.

CO-CREATING VALUE: THE PARTNERSHIP JOURNEY

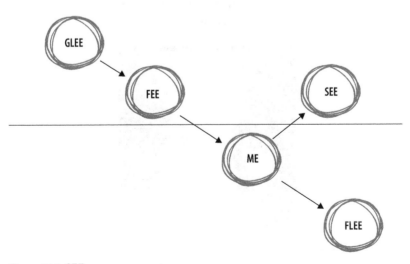

Figure 10.5: SEE

The starting point is to legitimise your partner or partners. Accept they're different and instead of focusing on the negative points of difference, start SEEing and appreciating the positive qualities and competencies they contribute.

Differences can be and are an incredible opportunity for growth; for creating something no individual with a single perspective can create. The way we deal with our differences can either be destructive or constructive. The choice is ours. We can choose to be a victim and move below the line into a doom loop, or choose to move above the line into a growth loop with all its learning potential.

> Where two worlds collide is the greatest opportunity for growth.

> From you and me can come WE.

> Instead of choosing to FLEE, we can choose to FLY.

The best relationships abolish 'either/or'; the best relationships understand and use 'The Power of And.'

Yes, you might think you can do it alone, but don't kid yourself, the journey won't be an easy one and the results will never match those you could achieve with the willing support of other people.

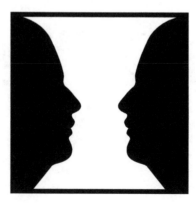

Figure 10.7: Chalice/faces[56]

The vase or chalice only exists because of both faces. Take one face away and the vase or chalice is gone. All relationships create some added value that neither individual can create alone. This means that the relationship which the parts have to each other is a part in and of itself; it's not only a part, but it's the most empowering, most unifying and most exciting part. It's unfortunate that in evaluating a relationship we most often don't see this value, only realising it was there once it's gone.

In effective relationships, the interdependent value created is so enormous that it both becomes and defines the relationship. It's like a third party made up of part me and part you, blending into something that's neither me nor you but totally unique with an incredible enriching value. It's not Either/Or, but the 'Power of And.'

&

When this happens the relationship supports both individual and partnership vision, values and needs, while *creating value that couldn't be created by any individual working alone. The best antidote for the FEE or ME stages of a relationship is to constantly see the value we can create.*

The relationship is now in the ultimate stage of WE:

CO-CREATING VALUE: THE PARTNERSHIP JOURNEY

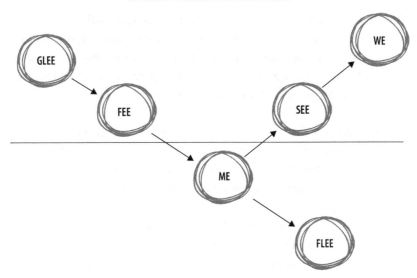

Figure 10.9: WE

The ingredients of WE:

1. Shared vision and common values that create alignment.

2. Win/win intention that creates a positive environment.

3. Ongoing conversations that stimulate creativity, building bridges and growth and creating 'The Power of And.'

Side bar: Assessing important relationships

Draw the above sketch on a landscaped flipchart page or on a window (use a whiteboard marker so you can easily wipe it off). Write the name of each important relationship, personal or business, on a post-it note and stick it on the sketch according to the current state of the relationship. This is an eye opening exercise. Choose the two priority relationships you would like to move to WE. Read the notes below and then write down the actions you are going to take to achieve your objective. Remember, it's a journey. Don't be impatient. Take it one step at a time, never forgetting why you're doing this and what you want to achieve.

1.   Shared vision and common values

While both partners must be true to who they are (personal arrows), they need to create a shared vision and common values (partnership arrow) to get to WE. This doesn't mean forsaking either of your personal Leadership Arrows. No! It's about legitimising each other's purpose, vision and values, and from these creating common purpose, vision and values.

A good example of this is when two strongly independent people marry and create a higher level family purpose, vision and values – an Arrowhead that holds them together through thick and thin, while simultaneously allowing them to flight their own personal arrows. Independence must be validated before interdependence can happen. "I will respect who you are, your desires and what you stand for, and you will respect who I am, my desires and what I stand for." I'm ok and you're ok. Only when this happens can we build a relationship that can create what we as individuals can never achieve.

Successful relationships require all parties to feel their needs are legitimate. This is the challenge of Leadership – to tap into common values. To do this, any leader must know and understand their followers. That's why it's not good enough to expect that people must do what they should 'because that's what they're paid for.' Success requires people to do more than they're paid for. Success requires people to use proactive initiative when faced with the unexpected, by taking action that aligns with 'the way we do things around here', leading to sustainable results. If we want people to lead themselves and not have to be managed then we must get their commitment to shared vision and values and inspire them using these.

"Few, if any, forces in human affairs are as powerful as a shared vision and shared values."

Peter Senge[55]

2.   Win/win intention

This ensures that all parties feel there are adequate wins for them in the relationship.

When one person feels they're consistently on the losing end of a relationship it will always lead to lose/lose. In today's interdependent world the only sustainable approach in any relationship, whether it's personal or business, is a win/win approach. Anything less than win/win might result in a short-term success, but it's not sustainable. You might win the battle, but will most likely lose the war.

"This is all very well," say many managers, "but you can't always give your employees a win. Circumstances just don't allow it." I hear the same from partners and parents. However it's important to realise that win/win is not only a result; it's an honest intention that strives to create win/win situations wherever possible. It's not a tactic or ploy. It's a value. A way of being. It's who you are and what you stand for. And always remember that Leadership is not what you do but who you are.

> ➤   Win/win is a philosophy, a value, an approach. Even if the final answer ends up being a compromise, the spirit of win/win leaves people feeling ok and more likely to act on the final agreement.

> Win/win is vital if any personal or business relationship has a chance of creating added-value.

I know it's hard to always achieve a win/win. What's important is that all parties feel they're striving for a win/win solution, and all concerned have really worked hard to try and achieve a win for each other.

In order to achieve win/win it's important that both/all parties really listen to each other. After all, how can I know what a win is for my partner if I don't listen and genuinely try to understand? Why this is so difficult for many people is because if they really try to understand another point of view or another opinion, they might in the process have to challenge their own thinking and change. In this way, striving for a win/win can be transforming and lead to change and growth. This is why the bottom of the Shaft of a high quality arrow (the blue zone) is flexible. It has to have some bend in it and in the same way our behaviour needs to have some flexibility in order to create win/win solutions.

Some clients have their employees make up vision boards depicting their own personal goals and values and their own Arrowhead, and then they have conversations about how helping the company achieve its purpose and vision will help them to achieve their own purpose and vision. Again striving for win/win.

That's Leadership.

Because people will never follow if they feel you're winning and they're losing. That's why the spirit of win/win can never exist in an environment of competition and contests.

The 2014 platinum miners' strike that continued for months on end with serious negative implications for all parties involved is an example of win/lose attempts that eventually became lose/lose.

> The miners lost many months of salary leaving them in dire financial straits.

> The mines lost production and profit.

> The City of Rustenburg, which once had one of the highest growth rates for a city in South Africa, was sent into a downward spiral of economic despair.

> South Africa was negatively impacted through downgraded growth projections and an unprecedented weakening of its currency.

> Many miners eventually lost their jobs and their lives.

And all this happened because parties were focused on seeing how they could preserve their own interests. In the end striving for a personal win became a lose/lose. A win/win solution could have been for the mines to provide a win for the miners by giving them the wage increase they were demanding. The miners in return could have given the mines the financial returns they were looking for by increasing productivity. I am sure this solution was discussed but *where was the leadership to bring this about? Where was the leadership to create 'WE'?*

3.   Ongoing conversations stimulate growth, creativity, bridge building and create the 'Power of And.'

Valuing the differences – mental, emotional and psychological – between two or more people is the essence of the 'Power of And',

and the key to valuing those differences is to realise that all people see the world, not as it is, but as they are.

If I believe I see the world as it really is, then why would I even consider your view point? I would see my version as being the reality. When people operate from this belief they can never be effectively interdependent. They can never get to WE. Unfortunately this is the state power so often creates – a one-sided view of reality that when acted on creates a win/lose situation. When we are left with our own perceptions, we constantly suffer from a shortage of data.

> The only way to overcome this one-sided perception trap we can so easily fall into is with ongoing conversations. When I become aware of

the difference in our perceptions or viewpoints, I say "Great! You see it differently! I value your opinion. Help me to see what you see." By doing this, I not only increase my own awareness, but I also affirm you. I validate your opinion, reducing the possibility of defensiveness and encouraging deeper conversation and understanding, allowing us to create the 'Power of And.'

Suggestions

Think of a person who sees things differently to you in a current situation:

➤ How could you incorporate these views into your thinking?

➤ How could you challenge your own thinking by considering these views?

This is where mindful awareness helps. By watching your own reactions to your thoughts and feelings and not acting blindly on them, you create more 'bend' in your arrow. So, for example, if you are confronted with someone who sees things differently to you and you have thoughts/feelings about this, you can watch your own reaction with curiosity and openness and then respond wisely based on common purpose and vision. At times like this always lead from the intention of your Arrowhead.

Communication: The vital ingredient

It was one of those warm, beautiful spring days. I was facilitating a strategy workshop at a resort in the Magaliesberg. During the mid-morning break I decided to have my coffee outside in the sun. I walked over to a koi fish pond where a man was busy sprinkling what I presumed to be food into the water. When I got to the edge of the water I noticed how incredibly beautiful the fish were. I approached the man and commented that these had to be the most beautiful Koi I'd ever seen. I remarked he must really look after the fish to get them like this.

"It's not about the Koi," he said, "it's about the water."
"The water?" I queried.
"Yes, the water," he replied. "There has to be enough water. If there isn't enough water it will stunt their growth. And the water needs to be clear. There also

needs to be appropriate nourishment in the water for the fish to feed on. And equally important, there can be no toxins in the water.

"Yes," he reiterated, "it's not about the fish, it's about the water."

I walked away from him wondering, "What if communication is to humans as water is to fish?" Communication is the medium through which relationships are made, and equally so, are destroyed.

There needs to be enough communication.

Only through enough communication can we:

➤ truly learn about ourselves and about each other

➤ begin to know each other's story, what people think and how they feel

➤ discover what a win is for our followers and partners

➤ solve problems

➤ grow a relationship

➤ effectively lead ourselves and others

Unfortunately, for so many reasons, when we try to have a conversation and it fails we replace conversation with silence. Why?

Because we think and feel it's safer. Speaking up carries with it too much of a risk, so we don't speak up when we need to. We sit on unresolved issues and resentment starts building up. We move below the happiness line to ME; we feel like a victim and we enter the doom loop.

Communication needs to be clear and this can only happen when:

➤ you have the courage to speak up so others can know your story

➤ you believe that listening to people is important and worth taking the time

➤ you believe everyone has something valuable to say

➤ you care enough to listen to truly understand the other's story

➤ you take the trouble to clarify understanding

So clarify, clarify, clarify, and the way to clarification is through good listening skills. Allow the speaker to finish what they are saying. Don't interrupt. When they're finished speaking clarify what you have understood by summarising your understanding. This will give the speaker the opportunity of correcting you or maybe even adding to the message to make it clearer. This way you will end up with as clear an understanding as possible. You and the speaker will be on the same wavelength.

The communication needs to be nourishing which can only come from:

➤ legitimising the other's point of view, even if you disagree with it

➤ always striving to achieve win/win resolutions

➤ giving someone genuine positive feedback

Think of the word 'nourishment.' What does it bring to mind?

Feeding. Enriching. Growing.

This is exactly what good communication does.

It feeds a relationship.
It enriches a relationship.
It grows a relationship.

There must be no toxins in the communication.

The way we communicate can leave a problem that can exist long after the content of this communication is forgotten. This can result from:

➤ attacking the person rather than the issue

➤ name calling

➤ allowing your emotions to control the communication

➤ putting people down

Great leaders know it's not only about what you say that matters; it's how you leave people feeling that counts.

At the end of the day, **THE COMMUNICATION IS THE RELATIONSHIP...**
NO COMMUNICATION, NO RELATIONSHIP.

Summary

1. Whether you're trying to lead yourselves or others, you can't succeed without the support of other people.

2. Getting people to want to support and follow you is the essence of Leadership.

3. People will only follow you if you inspire them, because they like where you're going, who you are (shared purpose, vision and values) and if they feel you accept them as they are – even if they're different.

4. This enables creativity, builds bridges, and leads to win-win relationships or partnerships that co-create value beyond that which any individual alone can create.

5. To achieve this, your own Arrowhead must be well defined and clearly communicated.

"Anger, resentment and jealousy doesn't change the heart of others – it only changes yours."

Shannon L. Alder[57]

Chapter 11

AVOIDING LEADERSHIP SUICIDE

"The best revenge is to be unlike him who performed the injury."

Marcus Aurelius[58]

One of my clients told me the following story that happened in her company. The Sales Director approached the National Sales Manager in October and told her he was going to retire, which would be announced the following February at the company's AGM. This meant the National Sales Manager would be promoted to Sales Director and she was told her help was needed to choose the next new National Sales Manager.

There were two obvious candidates for the job – Mr A, regional sales manager in the Western Cape, and Mrs B, regional sales manager in KwaZulu Natal. Upon discussion they realised either could get the position as both were ideal.

The criteria for choice would come down to the fact that both would be told they had three months where they would be put under a magnifying glass to really see if one of them exhibited something that would be a determining factor.

On her next trip around the country the National Sales Manager invited Mr A for a drink after work and told him the story – that the decision was between him and Mrs B. It came down to who would shine after three months. The next day she went to Durban and told Mrs B the same story. She told them both that at the end of the three months it could be their level of sales performance that might differentiate one from the other, so they should concentrate on delivering outstanding performances.

The next day Mr A arrived at work and met with the three sales consultants under him, who all had junior sales people reporting to them. He told each one, "Listen, if I go through there will be a vacancy in my position – and one of you could get the job. Our sales in the next three months can make the difference." They relayed the same message onto their junior salespeople and now the team was highly motivated. The carrot was dangled right in front of them. It now became about the right attitude motivating the right action.

It was decided that instead of their normal Friday afternoon meetings they should rather go out selling and have the meetings from 7am to 8am on Tuesday and Thursday mornings, which everyone committed to. They agreed to 'up their targets' and even did additional calls on a Saturday morning.

With that kind of attitude and activity what happened to the results after one month? The sales graph pointed upwards. The positive results reinforced their positive attitude which motivated them to continue the process.

Now they looked at where they could get more business from existing clients and new business from new clients. They were based in an office building in the centre of town and they noticed there was a company two floors above them which could be a potential customer. This client is now one of their biggest clients in the Western Cape.

After three months their results were outstanding and the day came where Mr A had to fly to Johannesburg for the AGM at which the choice of National Sales Manager would be announced. Now he normally left his car at the airport but this was a special day and his wife drove him to the airport, wished him luck and kissed him goodbye. On the plane there was an interesting talkative person sitting next to him and as a result the two hour flight felt like twenty minutes.

A company car met him and he arrived at head office half an hour before the meeting started and had coffee with his colleagues. His awareness was so open – he asked how their golf was going, how their families were. Ten minutes before the meeting was due to start the National Sales Manager asked him to come into her office so they could chat before the meeting began. Mr A thought, 'Yes, this is it!'

The National Sales Manager said, "I think you need to know before we go in that this was a very tough decision to make. Both of you are ideally suited for the job but we've decided to give the job to Mrs B. Her recent performance has really been outstanding."

Now suddenly all activity comes to a standstill. The rug has been pulled out from under him. His palms become sweaty, his mouth goes dry and his stomach is in a knot. He manages to say, "Well, Mrs B is an excellent choice and she'll do a good job." What's happened to his awareness? He hears nothing at the meeting. After lunch and a few glasses of wine the company car takes him back to the airport to catch his flight home. This time around he has no desire to talk to his fellow passengers. He wants to put the seat back and sleep.

What does his wife know instantly he walks into the arrivals hall? Her opening words: "You didn't get the job did you?" Once they're on the freeway home she launches into, "That bloody company, I warned you. I told you they'd use you and abuse you – and the kids, they don't know they have a father any more. I haven't got a husband any more. All you know is work and meetings." And meanwhile she's thinking what she's going to tell the book club girls.

When he arrives at work the next day a champagne breakfast is all laid out for a celebration. He says, "Guys, they gave the job to Mrs B but you deserve a celebration. You pulled out all the stops and you deserve it. I've come back with a whole lot of work to do, reports and stuff, so I'll be in my office." He goes into his office, closes the door and sits behind the desk.

This is when the first of the 3Rs set in. He's seething with resentment.

"Bloody company – how can they do this? After all I've given this company!" A short while later one of his salesmen comes in. "We've finished breakfast, can we get on with the morning's meeting?"

He replies, "I told you, I've got work to do, carry on without me."

The second of the 3Rs sets in… resistance.

At the end of the month when the branch is back to normal – with sales to match, no Saturday work, and Friday afternoon meetings reinstated, the third of the 3Rs kicks in. Revenge.

Against whom?

The company, he thinks!

Just as a virus can contaminate and even destroy software, and at times hardware, so there's one frequently used response to life that not only contaminates our personal software, but has the potential to permanently destroy relationships and even our health. This is possibly the most negative set of choices we can make on life's journey, and the most frightening thing is that when we use this response to life and others, we don't even realise it.

And in the process we are committing Leadership Suicide

I call it **The Deadly 3Rs**

Why the deadly 3Rs? Because it can kill you and any Leadership faster than a daily dose of poison.

Another triumph for the tramp. He has such a sly way of making us feel the 3Rs response is justified.

This response usually rears its ugly head when a relationship drops below the happiness threshold. I think I'm losing or paying too much for what I'm getting out of this relationship or situation. I think I'm on the losing end in this deal. I lose sight of the value that we can create and focus on me. These thoughts lead to the first of the 3Rs, **resentment**, and they dip me below the line into the victim or doom loop.

As the feelings of resentment build up with the 'feeling sorry for myself', 'hard done by', or 'angry' thoughts I replay over and over in my mind, so they start impacting on my behaviour, and the second of the 3Rs rears its ugly head, **resistance.**

I now start resisting the person or situation, avoiding it whenever possible, and instead of moving toward it, which is what I should be doing, I resist, move away and resentment builds, eventually leading to the third of the 3Rs, **revenge.**

The deadly 3Rs

Nations

You can switch on TV and see 3Rs between countries. Greeks and Turks; Palestinians and Israelis; America/allies and ISIS. In South Africa it's some blacks and some whites.

One nation or people doing something that another doesn't like or agree with, or having something the other wants. Resentment leading to resistance and ultimately revenge. Wars, World Trade Centre, racism, terrorism...

Families

You can get 3Rs between two families. The one family resents something the other has done or achieved. Resistance starts creeping in and eventually revenge happens. People not talking to each other and friendships ending.

You get 3Rs within families. Parents not talking to children or vice versa. I've seen this unfortunate situation so often.

When the kids are young they listen to you. They wear your kind of clothes, have your kind of friends, study what you want them to study. Now they're grown up they don't listen to you any more, want to wear their kind of clothes, choose their own friends, what they want to study and most definitely who they want to marry.

Resentment: *"After all I've done for the child, all the sacrifices I've made. Is this the appreciation I get?"*

Resistance: *Silence. Communication shuts down. Stewing.*

Revenge: *Silence can turn to violence/arguing/fighting. "Don't expect any help from me", or even, "I'll cut you out of my will."*

The closer and more important the relationship, the more vulnerable we become, the more chance of being hurt by others' actions. Note the saying, 'Familiarity breeds contempt.' That's why families are a fertile breeding ground for 3Rs.

Job or career

We resent the work we have to do, the inadequate and unfair pay we receive for the amount of responsibility we have, the way we're micro managed, the policies of the company and the disempowerment we feel. The possibilities for resentment are endless, leading to resistance and then revenge. Doing the bare minimum. Not being prepared to go the extra mile, eventually not even caring for company assets – even resorting to go slow or sabotage.

Customers or suppliers

The injustice of paying for something and then receiving shoddy service or poor delivery on promises, or the perceived excessive demands of customers threatening to go elsewhere if their demands aren't met.

Governments or politicians

Resentment because of political decisions or the power/greed of politicians and the impact it has on our lives. Corruption. Increased taxes. Not providing services for taxes paid. In South Africa this is so prevalent, with large numbers of all sections of the population having 3Rs toward government for not providing adequate education, security and even basic services in many areas.

Resistance builds up, ultimately leading to revenge. Severe criticism directed at government and politicians, especially by those taxed most heavily or those who gave their vote to the government in return of a promise of a better life. Marches, strikes, violence, often leading to immigration. Sometimes even wars.

Behaviour or actions of other people

If another can anger you then you are off balance with yourself. To regain your balance go back into the Arrowhead... your intention.

Note what can happen when someone cuts you off on the freeway.

RESENTMENT: "How dare you do that to me?" Or, "If I've got to obey the rules then who do you think you are to so blatantly violate them?" Or, "Listen idiot, the road doesn't belong to you." This is clearly an ego reaction, and where do these kind of thoughts lead? Resistance and ultimately revenge. Swearing, rude signs of our disgust designed to get back at the perpetrator. Cutting them off and then sitting in front of them as an 'I'll show you' reaction. And then possibly even road rage – revenge – leading to severe repercussions. When revenge becomes our purpose we are actually turning the arrow towards ourselves, shooting ourselves in the foot.

Reaction to our past

We resent events in our lives that happened in our past. Difficult childhoods, failed relationships, broken promises, having been taken advantage of. Events, which are now history, yet the emotional content remains so strong we simply can't let go. They prevent us from living fully, immobilising us in the present and creating worry about the future. Totally below the line. Here, once again, practicing a technique like mindfulness can help us to recognise when we are getting caught up in past patterning and feeling resentful, and then accepting our uncomfortable feelings of resentment rather than reacting mindlessly to them.

The 3Rs are a downward spiral to destruction. **It's like taking poison and waiting for the other person to die.** We're poisoning ourselves. It infiltrates all our thinking and feeling. It takes us right into a doom loop.

The only thing we get from responding with 3Rs is ego satisfaction.

"I showed her" – but I have damaged the relationship. "See if I care. I'll show my boss. From now on I'll do only what I'm paid for and no more" – but I don't have a future in this company anymore.

No. There's no argument that can justify the 3Rs. We must accept how negative and poisonous they are.

Why do we so often react with these deadly 3Rs? Our self-image will determine our degree of vulnerability and the tramp uses the 3Rs to protect us from our inner doubts, fears, insecurities and feelings of being taken advantage of, or being treated unfairly – feeling like a victim.

We're most vulnerable to the 3Rs when we fall beneath the happiness threshold – when we become focused on 'Me' and what this is costing 'Me.' The greater the injustice perceived and the hurt felt, the deeper below the line we go and the stronger the 3Rs reaction.

Why did Mr A react with 3Rs? Not because of disappointment. Surely disappointment is a fact of life? We don't always get what we want. Not because he felt they made the wrong decision. Wrong decisions happen.

Mr A reacted with 3Rs because of his ego and damaged self-image. "How dare they do this to me!"

How could Mr A have reacted?

Remember the Principle of Choice; of personal accountability. It's not what happens that matters, it's how I choose to respond to it that will create my reality.

I don't have to react blindly and impulsively out of anger, hurt or based on what others might think. These all lead to living below the line, finger pointing and blaming, fanning the flames of the 3Rs. Instead I can respond, in a considered, conscious and mindful way. I can choose to stay above the line, accepting accountability and leading myself forward, in alignment with my Purpose, Vision and Values. I can get back to my Arrowhead.

Can you see how much more in control you feel as you read the last few sentences?

You're moving back above the line. Feels good, doesn't it?

Mr A could have referred back to his Arrowhead asking himself the following questions:

- Purpose
  - Why am I in this job?

- Vision
  - What am I working towards in my career?

- Values
  - What do I stand for?

Reacting with 3Rs is always a choice. Once we become aware of how we're choosing to react and the possible destructive consequences of our choice, it's possible to consciously decide to substitute new, more constructive responses. It's simply choosing to respond in a different way.

Mr A had only two constructive, above the line, choices:

1. He could have carried on unconditionally for 60 days.

    - He could have accepted how bad he felt about not getting the promotion; maybe even believed the directors hadn't made the right decision. Nevertheless he could have carried on unconditionally by asking for honest feedback regarding the rationale for the decision, and asking himself what the next best step for his career might be – all the while delivering with total commitment.

2. He could have quit.

> After considering his purpose and vision for his career, he could have decided that this was the time to move on. He was ready for growth. Mr B was a competent manager and would probably be there for many years, and there was no other career path open to him within the company.

The middle of the road route of 3Rs is destructive.

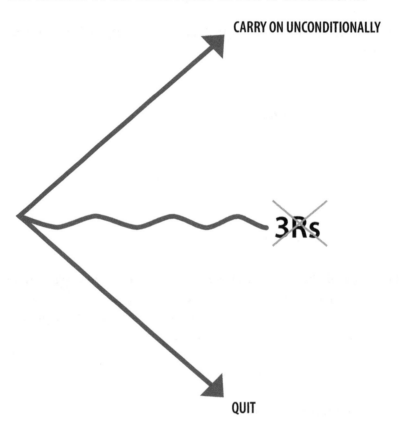

Figure 11.1: The 3Rs

After a talk I gave on this subject at a client conference a woman came up to me and told me a penny had dropped for her during my presentation. She had realised what a big 3R relationship she has with her husband and proceeded to unpack the details for me. Classic 3Rs: Resentment, Resistance and Revenge.

When she finished I asked her what she intended doing about it. She replied she wanted to carry on unconditionally. I then explained to her that carrying on unconditionally didn't mean going home to her husband and saying: "Wow, I heard this presentation today, and boy, do we have a 3R relationship, but don't worry because from now on I'm going to carry on unconditionally. Anything you want, anytime you want it, anyhow you'd like it, you've got it." No! That's not carrying on unconditionally. That's being a servant, a slave, a doormat.

Carrying on unconditionally means firstly accepting the principle of choice: that *you* choose to be in the relationship or the situation you're in.

You are not chained to your situation, you're free to leave.

I've had numerous debates with people on this. One woman told me she couldn't leave her husband because of financial considerations and for the well-being of her children, who were both severe asthmatics and would suffer unnecessarily through a divorce. I helped her see that in fact she was free to go if she chose to, but after considering her circumstances she chose to stay. It was her choice, even if not the most ideal choice. It was *her* choice.

A client once argued with me that, as unhappy as he was, he couldn't leave his job. There were numerous reasons why. Getting another job with his current financial package, giving him financial security when his children were at critical and expensive stages of their education was his main concern. Again, I helped him realise that staying in his current job was a choice he'd made after considering all options. A conscious choice he had to accept accountability for.

Carrying on unconditionally means once you accept the fact that you choose to be in a situation (accountability), you very quietly go about being the best: wife, partner, friend, parent, employee, manager you can be, allowing your behaviour (your Shaft) to be determined by your vision for the relationship (your Arrowhead), rather than being determined by the protectiveness and ultimate destructiveness of your tramp.

And why should you carry on unconditionally? Who do you owe it to? Not to the other person. No, *you owe it to yourself.* You have to look in the mirror daily and satisfy yourself you're doing a great job, you're a great partner, a value adding employee and contributing at your best possible level.

Carrying on unconditionally is a choice we make because we can *see* the value that can be created out of the relationship or the situation.

Carrying on unconditionally is initially a constructive step towards normalising a situation.

You're creating a more positive atmosphere. It reduces the emotional temperature in a situation. It's more conducive to constructive conversation happening.

Carrying on unconditionally is a choice we make because our purpose is to move to WE.

It implies a win/win relationship, so here's the critical part of carrying on unconditionally. Once the situation is normalised we need to initiate a constructive conversation that ensures both our needs are attended to. *This is not an event, it's a process which has to be managed on an ongoing basis. An ongoing journey. It doesn't happen after one conversation – it takes time.* That's why I say 60 days. You need to take confidence out of seeing meaningful progress, and all the while your self-esteem is growing because *you're putting yourself in control of the situation rather than allowing the situation to control you.*

Carrying on unconditionally is the only way I know you can transform a relationship or situation.

It's the only way to move from a win/lose to a win/win. It's the only way to get to WE.

If you carry on unconditionally in the way I've suggested and after time feel you aren't transforming the situation, then you still have the choice to stay and continue the process or make the other healthy above the line choice – to **Quit.**

It's important to remember that carrying on unconditionally is not just turning the other cheek. While you totally commit yourself to the relationship or the situation by delivering the best you can, you need to initiate conversations that clearly communicate what you're unhappy about, with the idea of finding win/win solutions.

Carrying on unconditionally is not about accepting a lose/win situation. Carrying on unconditionally creates the most conducive environment for constructive, above the line, win/win conversations to happen. Carrying on unconditionally is vital for Leadership. Trying to lead – by implication trying to influence someone to follow you – is impossible if you're tainted with the 3Rs. Having the 3Rs is like committing Leadership suicide.

Move your focus from short-term to longer term

The first step in dealing with the 3Rs is to move your focus from the short-term to the longer term; move from the Shaft of the arrow to the Arrowhead.

Resentment is usually a reaction to a current event; focus instead on your Arrowhead. Ask yourself why you're here, whether it's in a job situation or a relationship. What's your vision for this situation? What is the ideal outcome you'd like to achieve? Then reflect on your values. If you align your reaction to your Arrowhead and your values it will give you a far better perspective.

A CEO I was coaching had developed deep resentment to his board as a result of their decision-making that he felt hindered his ability to execute the business strategy. Resistance was already visible in his communication with the board and the situation was deteriorating rapidly He felt like a victim and was clearly below the line. I asked him a simple question – "Why are you here?", to which he answered, "It offers me a perfect springboard to the next phase of my career."

Stay Above the Line

I suggested we move above the line and look at his accountability in this situation. He reflected on this and then said that possibly he hadn't been assertive or persuasive enough in selling his strategy to the board, eventually suggesting that maybe his proposals to the board might lack the thoroughness needed to build confidence in his thinking.

In addition he agreed that simply reacting with 3Rs must be reflecting negatively in his interaction with the board, making matters worse and certainly damaging his credibility. As we discussed this he admitted that digging his heels in with the 3Rs had probably prevented him from listening and giving due consideration to the board's recommendations, which could have some merit. He re-focused on his Arrowhead, asking himself some accountability questions like, "What is this testing in me?" and "What do I need to do to transform this situation?"

A month later the feedback I got from him was extremely positive. To quote my client: "Nick, you helped me move from my ego to my Arrowhead, and I have found a way forward the board agrees with."

Note that he'd begun to carry on unconditionally, maximising his chance of success, but if at any time along the way this wasn't working, he'd have been free to choose to quit. This choice would then be easy because he wouldn't be doing it from the irrationality of 3Rs, but rather from the power of his purpose.

A self-fulfilling prophecy

So often I've seen the negative effects of having the 3Rs in a relationship, whether personal or in business. The outcome is usually a self-fulfilling prophecy, and is the antithesis of leadership.

A manager has 3Rs with someone who reports to him making it impossible for the individual to succeed. The subordinate is eventually forced out, goes elsewhere and flourishes.

A business owner has 3Rs with a particular client and eventually won't deal with that client, feeding his ego but not serving the business purpose.

A husband has 3Rs with his wife over a particular issue. The 3Rs impacts his overall attitude towards her, pushing the relationship below the happiness line to 'ME' or even to 'FLEE.'

The destructive negativity of the 3Rs lies in the fact that they're usually a response to a particular situation, which then, like a cancer, quickly spreads into the whole body of the relationship.

This was so vividly demonstrated in the movie *The War of the Roses*, when Kathleen Turner says to Michael Douglas, her screen husband: "I can't stand the way you chew your food."

Exercise

Think of a current or 3R situation you have in your life.

➤ Ask yourself; why am I here? Why is this relationship important to me?

➤ List the reasons you've reacted with 3Rs. The reasons that make you feel like a victim being taken advantage of.

It's so easy to focus on the victim side of the story while filtering out the accountable facts that point to our own role in creating our circumstances.

➤ Think of the other side of the story. List your own actions or inactions that could have contributed to your circumstances. What facts of the story have you conveniently left out? Remember that wherever we find ourselves in life, it's because of something we do or don't do.

➤ Now think of your purpose in this situation as you answer the question: Am I going to continue unconditionally, or quit?

➤ If you decide to quit, decide when and how.

➤ If you decide to carry on unconditionally, clarify your vision for the relationship – what you want to achieve, and ask an accountability question like: What's the very best next thing I can do to move me towards my vision?

➤ Stay above the line, keep learning, keep growing and always keep your Arrowhead top of your mind as you journey towards your purpose.

It's what great leaders do – they lead from their Arrowhead.

And there is no place in the Arrowhead for the poison called 3Rs.

In 1964 Nelson Mandela was arrested and brought to court to face an apparent death sentence for treason. He made a statement from the dock:

"During my lifetime I have dedicated myself to the struggle of the African people. I have fought against white domination and have fought against black domination. I have cherished the ideal of a democratic and free society in which all persons can live together in harmony and with equal opportunities. It is an ideal which I hope to live for and to achieve, and it is an ideal for which I am prepared to die."

He was sentenced to life imprisonment and over the years frequently rejected offers to be released if he would renounce his beliefs. He refused, and when released he spoke not from the bitter resentment of the 3Rs but in the language of reconciliation:

Comrades and fellow South Africans, I greet you all in the name of peace, democracy, and freedom for all.

His Arrowhead dipped deep into the psyche of the nation. It connected with the future that the majority of South Africans wanted. And they followed him.

Nelson Mandela had every reason to be indefinitely imprisoned by the anger of the 3Rs. Yet he came out of 27 years imprisonment with his Arrowhead defined and clear, never letting his circumstances overshadow his purpose, vision and values. Was he weak in not taking a revengeful ego-driven stand?

History gives us a clear answer.

Remember, Leadership comes from the root words meaning 'Feet' and 'To go first.'

Another origin of the word 'lead' is the ancient word leden, which means "To die for."

If you always think bigger picture or longer term and act accordingly, you will be on your way to Leadership.

The 3Rs and Leadership cannot live side by side.

Chapter 12

LEADERSHIP COMMUNICATION: STORIES THAT "STICK"

"To hell with facts! We need stories."

Ken Kesey – Author: *One Flew over the Cuckoo's Nest*[59]

"There's nothing more demoralising than a leader who can't clearly articulate why we're doing what we're doing."

James Kouzes and Barry Posner[60]

"A story can go where quantitative analysis is denied admission: our hearts."

Harrison Monarth[61]

If you could communicate your purpose, vision and strategy with impact, wisdom and memorability, what difference would that make to your influence as a communicator? What difference would it make to others' perception of you as a leader? A motivator? A parent?

In business, if your team were to share your purpose, vision, values and your strategy, how much easier would it be to drive your business forward? You and your team or family would be operating as one in the WE phase, moving with confidence and commitment towards a common goal. So consider the question, what do the following teachers, artists, and leaders all have in common? Jesus, Buddha, Geoffrey Chaucer, Mahatma Gandhi, Winston Churchill, Albert Einstein, Milton Erickson, Stephen Covey, Desmond Tutu and Nelson Mandela?

Answer: They all use(d) varieties of stories, anecdotes, parables, case histories and metaphors in order to put their message across in memorable ways.

A humorous way to look at this:

Following a fundraising dinner in New York, three holy men from three different religious communities were invited to give thanks. The story goes that the Christian priest offered a prayer about tolerance. The Muslim imam offered a prayer about charity. The rabbi, however, told a story, which contained a message for the diners to reflect upon. A week after the dinner, nobody could remember the prayers. But everyone could remember the rabbi's story and the power of its message.

Before the advent of modern technology, when the working day was done our ancestors used to gather around the fire and tell stories. Tales of the day's adventures, experiences and how they'd overcome challenges. They shared ancient tales of wisdom, learning and folklore.

Through their stories they made sense of their lives, created a shared sense of purpose and educated one another about their history, values and their destiny.

This was pure Leadership in action. Personal, connecting, emotional, impacting, transforming – Leadership communication through story telling.

Today we have more sophisticated technologies and yet the power of stories remains. We relate stories to our children, not only to keep them entertained but also to teach them about the world around them. We tell stories to friends over dinner to let them into our lives so they may know us better. And we tell stories at work in order to reinforce our culture or help people understand what is acceptable and unacceptable behaviour. Stories are a powerful and compelling way to transfer knowledge, information and understanding in a memorable way. Stories have the ability to break down barriers and turn bad situations around.

Stories dig deep into people's psyche and connect with their instinctive desires and needs in a way facts and figures never can. This is the way leaders connect their vision to the latent vision of others, as discussed in chapter 6. Stories draw out; they pull from the inside out while facts and figures push from the outside in.

This is the way that leaders infuse the Shaft with the purpose and direction of the Arrowhead.

Stories

Great leaders from Winston Churchill to Martin Luther King to Nelson Mandela have demonstrated that if you want people to follow you, if you want to transform a situation, then the voice is mightier than the sword.

Effective stories can change our opinions; they can inspire us to achieve goals we didn't think possible and motivate us to change things for the better.

Right now, executives and individuals around the world are sitting with the same questions: Why are we here? How did we get here? Where are we going? How are we going to create the change and commitment needed to get there?

These are all questions prompted by the Leadership Arrow and the answers can only come from stories.

Alexander Mackenzie, Programme Director of Storytelling at Cranfield University School of Management, said:

"The stories told around the boardroom table define the quality of leadership in the executive team. It's the leaders who connect the stories of the bigger picture, the vision, to their teams, that shape company culture and morale and it's the kind of stories told to clients and stakeholders that determine the deals made and delivered on."

This is not surprising, because good leaders have always been good storytellers. In the past decade storytelling has re-emerged as a leadership imperative, as indicated by the number of books and articles published, the prevalence of the theme at business conferences, and its inclusion as a subject of study in many business school curricula. Many companies utilise drama coaches to teach managers how to use the power of storytelling to increase their leadership quotient and communicate with influence.

University research increasingly points to the relevance of storytelling for improving both leadership and corporate success.

One of the most effective means I've used for developing Leadership in middle managers is to ask successful senior executives to share stories of their own Leadership journeys – stories that come from their own Leadership Arrows. Stories about their own purpose, vision and values. When I do this, the quality of attention in the room is quite amazing. These stories provide insight into how the senior leaders got to where they are, the challenges and hurdles they had to face, as well as insight into who these leaders are and what they stand for. It illustrates the openness and growth required to develop leadership ability more than traditional training alone can do. It's flesh and blood, and that's what Leadership is all about. It's not a façade! No! It's human, vulnerable, real and personal. After all, people ultimately follow you because of who you are.

During periods of change and evolution stories can be a powerful tool to help individuals adapt. By using the power of metaphor and analogy, leaders engage their audience, help them to overcome resistance, and leave them inspired to move forward towards a vision.

The purpose of Leadership stories is not to entertain. They have a specific goal or desired outcome they're trying to achieve.

The three states of effective stories

As Mackenzie says, stories should aim to deliver on three levels:

1. Inform: share intellectually what we know.
2. Engage: to communicate in a way that captures the attention of the audience.
3. Inspire: to stimulate imaginative curiosity.

Effective communication moves seamlessly and naturally between these three states.

Unfortunately, in the business environment we tend to get stuck in the first state – the realm of information. And yet research constantly confirms that the brain is like a sieve.

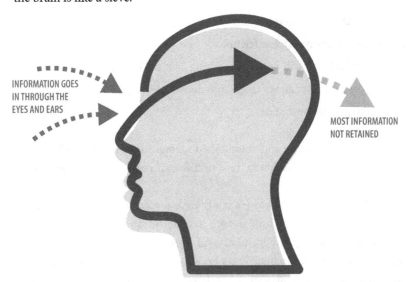

INFORMATION GOES IN THROUGH THE EYES AND EARS

MOST INFORMATION NOT RETAINED

Figure 12.1: The brain is like a sieve

This is why we forget data based information so quickly. In fact, it's widely accepted that the conscious brain can only hold up to seven pieces of information at a time. Add an eighth bit in and one of the original seven goes out. This is why in planning workshops all information is captured and made visible on flip charts or using sticky notes. We capture it, freeze it, and only then can we work with all of it.

The brain doesn't store information or words well. These are not 'sticky.' The brain stores associations, and when associations have an emotional dimension they become even more 'sticky.' All will agree that unemotional data is quickly forgotten. Fragments of information are forgettable. An emotional event, however, can be remembered for a lifetime.

We all know and remember the story of Little Red Riding Hood and the lessons that teaches about being aware of strangers – an example of a message that sticks. Relate it to a child once and with the emotional dimension high, the story sticks. Once is enough. Can you imagine trying to impart the lessons using a PowerPoint presentation, the preferred method of management communication?

Little Red Riding Hood: Five lessons for personal safety adapted from Jay Conger: *The Spotlight of Leadership*

1.   Be aware of strangers.
2.   They will always appear friendly.
3.   If you look you will notice something a bit off, e.g. big ears!
4.   People have a tendency to get into denial and to ignore warning signs.
5.   Do so at your own peril…

It certainly is a lot easier and at least it's documented. We can distribute it to all followers and refer back to it for 'I told you so' reasons, but it's not 'sticky.'

Let me back up a bit. Do stories really have a role to play in the business world? Believe me, I'm familiar with scepticism about them. When you talk about storytelling to a group of hard-headed executives, you have to be prepared for some eye rolling. That's because most executives operate with a particular mind-set. Analysis is what drives business thinking. It seemingly cuts through the fog of myth, gossip and speculation to get to the hard facts.

However, at a time when corporate survival often requires transformational change, Leadership involves inspiring people to act in new and often unfamiliar ways. Mind-numbing spreadsheets of numbers or sleep inducing PowerPoint slides won't achieve this goal. But effective storytelling often does. In fact, in certain situations nothing else works. Although good business cases are developed through the use of numbers, they are typically approved on the back of a story. Storytelling can translate dry and abstract numbers into a compelling leadership vision.

Effective leaders use the content of the Leadership Arrow to tell stories that build trust and influence followership. They tell stories reflecting the purpose, the vision and the strategy. Stories that will encourage followers to feel hope and happiness, helping them to see the hard work required in the Shaft of the arrow, is really worth the effort.

At Primedia Broadcasting, stories about LeadSA and the difference it's making in people's lives are communicated on a regular basis. In addition, employees are often involved in 'making a difference' initiatives, where they create the stories they are later proud to relate. This helps keep people in touch with the organisation's Arrowhead, giving meaning to the fast-paced and often pressurised daily work that needs to be done in the Shaft of the arrow in the course of a normal radio station day.

One of the top hotel groups in the world, Ritz Carlton Hotels, has at the tip of their Arrowhead their purpose: *"We are ladies and gentleman, who serve ladies and gentleman."* In order to internalise this, as part of their induction, all new Ritz Carlton employees are required on a daily basis for four weeks to document stories of employees living out the organisation's purpose, and then to relate these stories to their peers.

A client of mine's business had been through a period of bad results. At a staff meeting he wanted to boost their morale and inspire them to work harder to make up losses. Fortunately his story was recorded. Here's a transcript:

"When I started this company 10 years ago", he began, "I didn't know how to run a business. I figured I could do everything myself and succeed. I was dead wrong. I worked 15-hour days to keep up with it all. I wanted to grow the company, but quickly realised I didn't know how and that I couldn't do it alone.

"All of you know how stubborn I am so I tried to go it alone. But I started to lose clients because I couldn't keep my promises. I didn't have time to bid for work, so my competitors got ahead and I even lost some clients. This put enormous pressure on my family because I was never home. I knew that if things continued this way, the company would go under in a matter of months and that I might lose my family. I needed help.

"Once I realised I had to ask for help, I did. I put some major projects on hold and started to look for some great people to help me achieve my vision. I handpicked each one of you because you're the best at what you do. You all have the skills, knowledge and experience I lack. I believe in all of you and I believe that we will turn this problem around, so let's focus on our vision and think of how we can help each other succeed."

Telling stories is an important part of a leader's toolbox for communicating change.

"The best way to get humans to venture into unknown terrain is to make that terrain familiar and desirable by taking them there first in their imaginations."

Noel Tichy[62]

Effects of storytelling

Assessments of the effects of storytelling on performance have emerged. A study by Prusak[63] explored the experiences of some 40 companies undergoing major changes. All these programmes could potentially have had a large economic impact on the organisation and all required major companywide changes in behaviour, tasks and processes.

Two things were striking about the study's findings.

First, it's remarkable how little success the companies had with their change programmes. In all, 58% of companies failed to meet their change business case targets; 20% captured only a third or less of the value expected. The overall differences between the winners and losers were huge. The 42% successful companies not only gained the expected returns, but in some instances they exceeded them by as much as 200 to 300%.

Second, one of the key success factors was storytelling. Although there were a number of critical success factors, the researchers found a high correlation between storytelling and success.

Mackenzie[64] further compared the effectiveness of four different methods to persuade a group of MBA students of an unlikely hypothesis: that a company really practiced a policy of avoiding layoffs. In one method there was just a story. In the second the researchers provided statistical data. In the third they used statistical data and a story. In the fourth they offered a policy statement made by a senior company executive. The most effective method of all turned out to be the first alternative – telling the story alone.

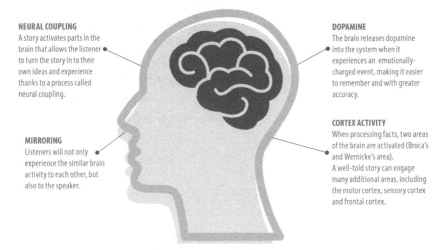

NEURAL COUPLING
A story activates parts in the brain that allows the listener to turn the story in to their own ideas and experience thanks to a process called neural coupling.

MIRRORING
Listeners will not only experience the similar brain activity to each other, but also to the speaker.

DOPAMINE
The brain releases dopamine into the system when it experiences an emotionally-charged event, making it easier to remember and with greater accuracy.

CORTEX ACTIVITY
When processing facts, two areas of the brain are activated (Broca's and Wernicke's area). A well-told story can engage many additional areas, including the motor cortex, sensory cortex and frontal cortex.

Figure 12.2: How storytelling affects the brain[65]

A client, SBV, which is the biggest movers of wholesale cash in South Africa, found itself operating in an environment where customers were demanding both increased and innovative service solutions. SBV had been and still was a highly successful business with a culture that encouraged long tenure amongst employees, many of whom who had spent their whole career with the company. CEO Grant Dunnington and his management team knew that much in the business had to change in order for them to align with new customer requirements. Previous change initiatives had met with the usual denial and resistance from the very loyal people who had so successfully used a proven but now outdated formula.

The Leadership team was concerned that employees would see change as a sign the business was no longer successful and that their jobs were at risk. Previously, change had been communicated via the usual e-mail and PowerPoint communications. This time, however, Grant decided to communicate with a story.

He started off telling a story reflecting the history and growth of SBV through the years; how it got to be the successful giant of a business it currently is. He continued by illustrating a parallel story – the development and growth of the iPhone to the dominant global player it is today. This coincided with the release of the iPhone 6, which was extremely topical at the time. In addition, being a mobile phone it was something all people found relevant and could relate to. They could connect.

He explained that SBV was just like the iPhone. It had to be upgraded to remain relevant. iPhone 6 didn't imply that the iPhone 5 was not successful – it was a huge winner as was SBV. But because of competition, Apple could not rest on its laurels and had to continually improve and upgrade. In the same way, SBV needed to upgrade. This analogy set the scene and gained the commitment for what proved to be two extremely constructive days of strategy planning.

"Storytelling has the power to transform change resistant organisations"

Steve Denning[66]

And it's not only leaders in business or politics who can benefit from a greater capability to use stories. Anyone who has a new idea or wants to create change will do better by telling stories than by offering any number of facts or reasons. It's equally applicable to school teachers, health workers, therapists, family members, and colleagues – in short anyone who wants to influence others.

How 'sticky' would the message I'm trying to communicate in this book be without the numerous stories, analogies and metaphors I've used? I'm sure most readers will remember the story of the tramp, the lessons from the guests at the braai, the analogy of above the line/below the line, and the Robben Island story long after cold information has been forgotten.

Here is another example of brilliant communication that 'sticks' and leads to change:

Haier, the Chinese home appliance manufacturer and a leader in its market space, is a state-owned company with three decades of business under its belt – an eternity in fast-moving China. Zhang Ruimin, its current chief executive officer, is widely credited with rescuing what was, in the 1980s, a dilapidated refrigerator company and turning it into a world-class organization. Ruimin is an innovator who had a vision for change that was based on quality improvement and process efficiency. To emphasise the need for change when the company was struggling and close to bankruptcy, Ruimin brought dozens of poorly made refrigerators down to the factory floor and distributed sledgehammers to employees. In a move that no one present would forget, he ordered workers to demolish the refrigerators and took the first swing himself. It was an iconic moment that defined the organization and established a corporate culture based on high standards and productivity. With the swing of the hammer he instantly changed the course of the organization.

That's how leaders communicate.

Jeffrey Sampler[67]

My purpose for including this topic is because I don't believe Leadership can happen without creative communication that:

> communicates who you are, what you stand for, shows your vulnerability and develops Leadership credibility

> inspires purpose and vision

> leads people into the future

> ingrains values

> fosters collaboration

> tames the grapevine

> communicates who your company is – branding

> encourages change

All I can do in this chapter is to convince you of the power of stories to create Leadership that attracts followers. We all have the ability to tell stories; we've been doing it since we learned to speak. We do it all the time at dinners, barbeques and all the other social gatherings that are part of our lives. I can only hope I've encouraged you to start experimenting and using this natural gift in your own Leadership journey. Like all skills, storytelling can be honed and perfected. A Google search will connect you with so many resources to help improve your storytelling ability.

➤ *Every leader a storyteller* – breathing brightness into business by Peter Christie

➤ *The virtuosa organisation: The importance of VIRTUES for a successful business* by Graham Williams, Dorian Haarhoff and Peter Fox

The main elements of a story

1. The idea being communicated by the story must be clear and worthwhile. Know why you're telling the story and what you want to achieve.

2. The story can be based on an actual example (Robben Island as an example of the power of shared vision) or an analogy or metaphor (the importance of water for Koi fish as a metaphor of the importance of conversations to humans). Note that the story must connect with what you want to achieve – point 1.

3. If it's a true story, give a date and place where it happened.

4. Choose a story your audience can relate to, e.g. iPhones and upgrades.

5. Keep it factual, simple and strip out unnecessary detail.

6. Have a positive ending or great quote.

7. Link the change idea to the story, e.g. what if conversation is to humans as water is to fish? It must be abundant, clear, nourishing, and non-toxic.

Tips to enhance your storytelling

➤ Tell your story as if you were talking to one person.
➤ Be yourself.
➤ Be rehearsed but spontaneous.
➤ Get out from behind the podium.
➤ Connect with all parts of the audience.
➤ Use gestures – be animated and lively.

➤ Use visual aids sparingly.

➤ Use and be comfortable with your own style.

I have used many stories in my attempt to illustrate the Leadership Arrow.

I hope these stories of my personal journey in life makes me real to you, the reader, giving you the opportunity to know me, who I am, and what I believe in.

PART FOUR:

LEADERSHIP – AN
ONGOING JOURNEY

Chapter 13

THE LEADERSHIP EDGE

"Life is like playing a violin solo in public and learning the instrument as one goes on."

Samuel Butler[68]

Many will agree that there is a fine line between winners and losers, between successes and failures, between those who are happy and those who are unhappy. Note the fractions of a second between winners and losers in sport. In golf, winners might win by a one or two shot difference in 216 shots. And winners have this slight edge – consistently.

It's no different in life or in business. Yet we place successful people on a pedestal. We see them as special, gifted, and talented. This is not the case. They are simply normal people, not normal people who know some 'success secret.' No, they are simply normal people who have an edge, and just as in sport, that edge is enough to make them winners in the contest that is life or business. So, what gives them that edge? Think of all the words used to describe successful people and you can summarise them into three phrases:

➤ Burning Intention – The Arrowhead

➤ Driven Execution – The Shaft

➤ Unwavering Stability – The Fletchings

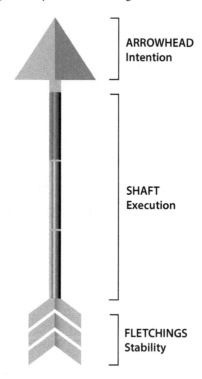

Figure 13.1: The Leadership Arrow

If any one of these is missing, success is short-term and not sustainable. List life's casualties and you will always find at least one of the three parts of the arrow lacking.

➤ Enron – violation of values (Fletchings: Stability)

➤ Hitler – untenable purpose (Arrowhead: Intention)

➤ Kodak – no vision, wrong strategy (Arrowhead: Intention)

➤ Greece – wrong strategy (Arrowhead: Intention)

➤ Eskom – no long-term vision and weak execution (Arrowhead: Intention and Shaft: Execution)

➤ Tiger Woods – violation of values (Fletchings: Stability)

If you probe you will always find that successful people and businesses have a burning intention; they are driven by a sense of purpose. Some might not even be able to articulate it, but it's there as was discovered by the 'Why am I so unhappy group' from chapter 5.

So often I have counselled people, from individuals to CEOs, and helped them to identify their purpose. When they eventually see it, it is like a light bulb going on in their minds. One CEO said to me at her 'light bulb' moment, "Oh my God! Now I understand!"

Successful people also have a clear vision of what they want to achieve. They can see it, touch it and smell it, as if it were already happening. The great Gary Player knew this. When his son informed him that he wanted to follow in his footsteps as a professional golfer, Gary instructed him that at the next Sunday family dinner he should be prepared to make the speech he would make when he won his first major tournament. Gary really understood the power of vision. All great leaders ensure that followers understand *why* they do what they are required to do and that they have an inspiring vision of *where* they are going.

Successful people also have the discipline that comes from a clear, high level, long-term, strategy; a strategy that succinctly and simply defines *how* they are going to succeed; a strategy fuelled and driven by the passion flowing out of purpose and vision. It is this discipline that is seen as the intense drive and commitment that winners are always described as having. It is this discipline that provides the momentum for execution in the shaft. Take away purpose and vision and drive becomes diluted; commitment becomes convenience; 'want to' becomes 'have to.' And sure, this drive and commitment means that winners can be and are hard on themselves, because winning is not for sissies.

Leadership of others is no different. It's not the 'soft' stuff.

Effective leaders are tough because they are non-negotiable regarding their purpose, vision, values and high-level strategy. This longer-term focus provides the clarity of intention and consistency of message that any leader must have to be effective. It communicates what is important rather than what is urgent.

By implication, success means setting stretch goals. These take the leader and the followers right out of their comfort zone; their journey enters uncharted territory – very often territory for which no map has yet been drawn up. They are playing the symphony while still learning the violin! And that is why Leadership is essentially an inside job and why leadership development is really nothing other than personal development. It's about 'who you are.'

The inside must be right. It's the beginning of having 'the edge.' It requires self-understanding and learning how to effectively manage our own distinctive psychology – our own unique tramp.

It means developing a philosophy of living above the line, especially when those unexpected challenges and hurdles happen; and they will happen.

It means understanding the power that the privilege of choice affords us, and it means exercising that privilege within a context of clear intention created by personal purpose and vision and the stability of our values.

Yes, Leadership is a journey. There is no short cut. There are no '6 steps' or 'rules' for effective Leadership.

The only way to become a better leader is to know and understand yourself and then to get out there and lead, with the passion created by purpose, the vigour created by vision, the focus created by strategy, and the stability and sustainability provided by universal values.

Put these together and you have The Leadership Arrow.

Epilogue

Leadership is not about the target, it's about the flight

When the intention of the Arrowhead connects as one with the execution in the Shaft and the stability provided by the Fletchings, we experience that thing called 'flow' – also called 'being in the zone.' It's striving yet not-striving. It's effort yet it's effortless. Yes it's about scoring the goal, but it's also about getting lost in and loving the game.

The story was told of a young bird that was put in a cage with other birds. At first it incessantly flew against the bars of the cage trying to get out. Its owners consoled it, pointing out the advantages of easy food and water, a nice swing and the shiny mirror. Pretty soon the bird accepted its fate and stopped trying to get out. Then one day a large bird alighted on top of the cage and opened the cage door. Some of the other birds saw the open door and flew out, but our young bird didn't understand its meaning.

He had forgotten how to fly.

Flying means trusting that you have honed your arrow, pointed it in the right direction, and effortlessly let it go. All the lessons in this book take a certain amount of effort to acquire, but if you try too hard to achieve them you will be back with your tramp again, feeling doubtful and being too hard on yourself. So, to take flight, take a deep breath and know that if you are reading this book then you are already open to its lessons; just trust yourself and let your arrow fly.

If a bird thinks too hard about how to fly, it may never lift off the ground. A bird simply flies. The same with leaders. Leaders don't think too much about leading. They lead. So, absorb from this book whatever resonates with you. Live with it. Ponder it. Start building your own arrow. Try out some of the suggestions. But do so with a sense of curiosity and openness, and trust that you already have it in you to fly.

The celebration of arrival happens in the future, but the ecstasy of the flight happens now: Purpose. Perfection. Beauty. Adventure. Discovery. Flow.

Any way you describe it…
It's what human beings desire.
It's what great Leadership provides…
The opportunity to fly.

"Most gulls don't bother to learn more than the simplest facts of flight – how to get from shore to food and back again. For most gulls, it is not flying that matters, but eating. For this gull, though, it was not eating that mattered, but flight. More than anything else, Jonathan Livingston Seagull loved to fly."

Richard Bach[67]

Acknowledgments

I owe a debt of gratitude to so many people for the role that they played in making this book a reality. My biggest thank you goes to my wife Audrey, who believed in me, challenged me, motivated me, and kept me going when she saw the process slowing down, either because of pressure of work or because my own doubts made me wonder whether I could do it or not. I so appreciate her understanding and support when I spent so many weekends and holidays writing.

An equally big thank you to my daughter Anthea for all the inspiration, the typing and the re-typing. I must have written a thousand pages before getting to the final version, and she walked every step of the way with me – word for word. You are amazing.

Thank you to my son Paul whose creative writing ability has set an incredibly high standard for me and for his reviews and constructive comments along the way. You are so talented.

Thank you to my son-in-law Evan Sotiropoulos and Five0Six for all the help with the layout and graphics for the book. You are a design guru.

Thank you to Marion Scher for your editing and constructive comments. Your very presence put pressure on me to meet deadlines.

A very big thank you to Wilhelm Crous and Cia Joubert from Knowledge Resources for their professional approach, constructive comment and support as the book unfolded. It has been a pleasure having them on my side.

Thank you to all those clients who have travelled my own leadership development journey with me. I have worked with so many incredible CEOs and their management teams, some for many years, giving me the privilege of a longer-term view of leadership rather than a snapshot of leadership at a moment in time. They have trusted me with the wellbeing of their businesses, which has kept me learning and growing, providing much of the content for this book. Thank you all. Without the experiences that you afforded me, this would not have been possible.

Thank you to the late Sedley Berger for the opportunity he gave me to enter the consulting field and for introducing me to the concept of the 3Rs.

Special thanks to Dr Deon van Zyl for being part of my consulting journey at the time when I needed to accelerate my own development. The projects we did together really broadened my perspective and learning. You taught me the real value of diversity. I am waiting for your book.

Thanks to Katy Katapodis and Robin Wheeler for continuously prompting me to write this book, as well as all those clients who constantly urged me to document what I was teaching. I eventually got there.

So many other people have influenced my life and this book by their very presence and the example they have set.

> My siblings, Paul, Jimmy and Aster and their families.
> The Christelis family in South Africa and the USA.
> The Christodolides family
> The Sotiropoulos family
> The Leonards
> The late Evan Poulos
> Steve Griessel
> Liz Kobilski
> Terry Volkwyn
> Yusuf Abramjee
> Brett Archibald

You have all influenced who I am today. Please regard this book as a small 'Thank you.'

Finally, a very big thank you to James and Kathy – my wonderful, loving, generous, and always supportive parents.

References

Adizes, I. 1988. *Corporate Lifecycles: How and why corporations grow and die and what to do about it.* New York: Prentice Hall

Bach, R. 1970. *Jonathan Livingston Seagull the Story.* New York: Macmillan.

Barakat, C. 2014. *The science of storytelling (infographic).* [Online]. Available: www.adweek.com/socialtimes/science-storytelling-infographic/150296 [Accessed 24 July 2015]

Bhide, A. 1999. *The origin and evolution of new businesses.* Oxford: Oxford University Press.

BrainyQuote.com. 2015a. Carrie Fisher Quotes. [Online]. Available: http://www. brainyquote.com/quotes/quotes/c/carriefish384531.html. [Accessed 24 July 2015].

BrainyQuote.com. 2015b. Ken Kesey Quotes. [Online]. Available: http://www. brainyquote.com/quotes/quotes/k/kenkesey380260.html [Accessed 24 July 2015].

BrainyQuote.com. 2015c. Marcus Aurelius Quotes. *[Online]. Available:* http://www. brainyquote.com/quotes/quotes/m/marcusaure383110.html [Accessed 24 July 2015].

BrainyQuote.com. 2015c. Peter Marshall Quotes. [Online]. Available: http:// www.brainyquote.com/quotes/quotes/p/petermarsh382875. html#YQUYZs5TlvAEF0UE.99 [Accessed 24 July 2015].

BrainyQuote.com. 2015e. Robert South Quotes. [Online]. Available: http://www. brainyquote.com/quotes/quotes/r/robertsout186846.html. [Accessed 24 July 2015].

BrainyQuote.com. 2015f. Walt Disney Quotes. [Online]. Available: http://www. brainyquote.com/quotes/quotes/w/waltdisney130027.html. [Accessed 23 July 2015].

BrainyQuote.com. 2015g. William Jennings Bryan quotes. [Online]. Available: http:// www.brainyquote.com/quotes/quotes/w/williamjen389006.html, [Accessed 23 July 2015].

Clance, P. R. & Imes, S. 1978. The Imposter Phenomenon in High Achieving Women: Dynamics and Therapeutic Intervention. *Psychotherapy Theory, Research, and Practice,* 15(3), 1-8, 15, 241 - 247.

Coehlo, P. 2005. Eleven minutes. New York: Harper Perennial

Collins, J. C. (2001). Good to Great. New York: Harper Collins.

Conant, D. & Norgaard, M. 2011. *Transforming everyday interactions into powerful leadership moments.* ASTD lecture. Orlando, Florida.Concise

Confucius. 1870. "The Doctrine of the Mean," in *The Chinese Classics* by James Legge. New York: Hurd & Houghton. pp. 124-146. [Online]. Available: http://www.shsu.edu/~his_ncp/Confu.html [Accessed 23 July 2015].

Covey, S. R. 1989. *The 7 Habits of Highly Effective People.* New York, NY: Simon and Schuster.

Cranfield. 2015. *Storytelling is at the heart of leadership.* [Online]. Available: http://www.som.cranfield.ac.uk/som/dinamic-content/media/Praxis/Storytelling%20is%20at%20the%20heart%20of%20leadership.pdf [Accessed 24 July 2015].

Dean, K. W. 2008. *Values based leadership: how our personal values impact the workplace.* [Online]. Available: http://www.valuesbasedleadershipjournal.com/issues/vol1issue1/deanphp [Accessed 24 July 2015].

Denning, S. 2001. *The Springboard: How Storytelling Ignites Action in Knowledge-era Organizations.* London: Butterworth-Heinemann.

Doran, G. T. *1981.* There's a S.M.A.R.T. way to write management's goals and objectives. *Management Review, 70(11), 35-36.*

Drucker F. 2005. *Legacy advice from a wise man.* [Online]. Available: www.slideshare.net. [Accessed 24 July 2015].

Ellsworth, R.E. 2002. *Leading with purpose: the new corporate realities.* Stanford: Stanford University Press.

Ernest, P. 2001. *The values journey.* Keynote address: ASTD International Conference and Expo (Florida, USA).

Fineman, M. 1996. *The nature of visual illusion.* New York, NY: Dover, pp 111 and 115.

Frankl, V. E. 2004. *Man's search for meaning.* London: Random House.

Freud, A. 1946. *The ego and the mechanisms of defence.* New York, NY: International Universities Press.

Gottlieb, B.H. 1985. Social Support and the Study of Personal Relationships. *Journal of Social and Personal Relationships.* September, 1985 2: 351-375.

Good Reads. 2015. Louise Hay Quotes. [Online]. Available: http://www.goodreads.com/author/quotes/74538.Louise_L_Hay?page=2 [Accessed 23 July 2015].

Goshal, S. 2010. *The smell of the place.* [Online]. Available: http://www.youtube.com/watch?v=UUddgE8rI0E [Accessed 21 March 2013].

Hamel, G. 1997. *Killer strategies that make shareholders rich the top companies thrive, says our author a leading strategy guru by changing the rules of the game. [Online].* Available: http://archive.fortune.com/magazines/fortune/fortune_archive/1997/06/23/228085/index.htm [Accessed 23 July 2015].

Herrigel, E. 1953. *Zen in the art of archery.* [Online]. Available: http://www.ideologic.org/files/Eugen_Herrigel_-_Zen_in_the_Art_of_Archery.pdf [Accessed 23 July 2015].

Jansen Kraemer Jr., H. 2011. *The only true leadership is values-based leadership.* [Online]. Available: www.forbes.com/2011/04/26/values-based-leadership.html. [Accessed 24 July 2015].

Johnson, B. 1996. *Polarity Management, Identifying and Managing Unolvable Problems.* Amherst, Mass: HRDPress Inc.

Jung, C. 2001. *Modern Man in Search of a Soul.* Abingdon: Routledge.

Lapin, D. (2012). *Lead by greatness.* [Online]. Available: http://www. leadbygreatness.com. [Accessed 24 July 2015].

Lichtenstein, S. 2005. *Strategy co-alignment: Strategic, executive values and organisational goal orientation and their impact on performance* (Doctoral dissertation, Henley Management College). [Accessed 23 July 2015].

Lichtenstein, S. 2012. *The role of values in leadership: how leader's values shape value creation.* Available: http://integralleadershipreview.com/6176-the-role-of-values-in-leadership-how-leaders-values-shape-value-creation/ [Accessed 23 July 2015].

Mail & Guardian. 25 February 2015. Notes from the Design Indaba. [Online]. Available: http://mg.co.za/article/2015-02-25-notes-from-the-design-indaba-conference-day-2 [Accessed 24 July 2015].

Mintzberg, H. 1992. Five Ps for Strategy in *The Strategy Process.* pp 12-19, H Mintzberg and JB Quinn eds., 1992. New York, NJ: Prentice-Hall International.

Mintzberg, H., Ahlstrand, B. & Lampel, J. 2005. *Strategy bites back.* London: Financial Times/Prentice Hall.

Monarth, H. 2014. *The Irresistible Power of Storytelling as a Strategic Business Tool.* [Online]. Available: https://hbr.org/2014/03/the-irresistible-power-of-storytelling-as-a-strategic-business-tool/ [Accessed 24 July 2015].

Motivation for dreamers. n.d. Motivation Quotes. [Online]. Available: http://www. motivation-for-dreamers.com/motivation-quotes.html. [Accessed 23 July 2015].Munroe, M. 2003. The Principles and Power of Vision. *New Kensington, PA: Whitaker House*

Nathan, G. 2004. The franchise e-factor. Brisbane: Franchise Relationships Institute

Nelson, P. 1993. *There's a hole in my sidewalk: The romance of self-discovery.* Hillsboro, OR: Beyond Words Publications.

Nutt, P. C. 1984. Strategic planning network for non- profit organizations. Strategic *Management Journal, 5(1), 57 – 75.*

Ortberg, J. 2014. *If You Want to Walk on Water, You've Got to Get Out of the Boat.* Michigan: Zondervan.

O'Toole, J. 1996. *Leading change: the argument for values-based leadership.* New York: Ballantine Books.

Oxford English Dictionary. 12th edition 2011. New York, NY: Oxford University Pres⁵

Sampler, J. L. 2014. *Bringing strategy back: How strategic shock absorbers make planning relevant in a world of constant change.* London: John Wiley & Sons.

Search Quotes. 2015. Shannon Alder Quotes. [Online]. Available: http://www. searchquotes.com/quotation/Anger,_resentment_and_jealousy_doesn't_ change_the_heart_of_others...it_only_changes_yours./324705/ [Accessed 24 July 2015].

Senge, P. 1990. *The fifth discipline: The art and practice of the learning organisation.* New York: Doubleday. 206.

Sheehy, G. 2006. *Passages: Predictable crises of adult life.* New York: Random House LLC.

Taylor, S. 2012. *Back to Sanity. The healing of the Human Mind.* London: Hay House.

The Economist. 2 June 2009. Mission Statement. [Online]. Available: http://www.economist.com/node/13766375. [Accessed 23 July 2015].

Tichy, N. M. & Cohen, E. B. 1997. *The Leadership Engine: How Winning Companies Build Leaders at Every Level.* London: HarperBusiness.

ThinkExist.com. 2015. Maya Angelou quotes. [Online]. Available: http://thinkexist.com/quotation/nothing_will_work_unless_you_do/215802.html [Accessed 23 July 2015].

Tolle, E. 1997. *The Power of Now: A Guide to Spiritual Enlightenment.* [Online]. Available: http://www.baytallaah.com/bookspdf/51.pdf [Accessed 23 July 2015].

Waters, M. 2008. *Leadership values.* MBA Dissertation, Henley Management College/Brunel University.

Wikipedia. n.d.(a) Marikana tragedy. 16 August 2012. [Online]. Available: https://en.wikipedia.org/wiki/Marikana_killings. [Accessed 24 July 2015].

Wikipedia. n.d.(b) St Augustine of Hippo. [Online]. Available at: https://en.wikipedia.org/wiki/Augustine_of_Hippo. [Accessed 24 July 2015].

Wikiquote. n.d. Samuel Butler, Novelist. [Online]. Available: https://en.wikiquote.org/wiki/Samuel_Butler_(novelist). [Accessed 24 July 2015].

Wisdom Quotes. 2015. James Kouzes and Barry Posner Quotes. [Online]. Available: http://www.wisdomquotes.com/quote/james-kouzes-and-barry-posner-1.html [Accessed 24 July 2015].

Worth, M. J. 2009. *Nonprofit Management: Principles and practice.* Los Angeles, CA: SAGE Publications.

List of readings

Biehl, B. 1995. *Stop Setting Goals if you would rather solve problems.* Nashville, Tennessee: Moorings.

Chan, W. K. & Mauborgne, R. 2005. *Blue ocean strategy: How to create uncontested market space and make the competition irrelevant.* Boston: Harvard Business School Press.

Connors, R; Smith, T; Hickman, C. 2004. *The Oz Principle.* (USA). Penguin

Gallwey, W. T. 2000. *The Inner Game of Work.* New York: Random House.

Kay, J. 2010. *Obliquity: Why our goals are best achieved indirectly.* London: Profile Books.

Kets de Vries, M. 2001. *The Leadership Mystique: a user's manual for the human enterprise.* London: Financial Times/Prentice Hall.

Kouzes, J. M. & Posner, B. Z. 2007. *The Leadership Challenge.* (4th ed.). San Francisco: Jossey Bass.

Lapin, D. 2012 *Lead by greatness.* Smashwords Edition. [Online]. Available: http://www.leadbygreatness.com [Accessed 23 July 2015].

Mandela, N. *20 April 1964.* Statement from the dock at the opening *of the defence case in the Rivonia Trial.* [Online]. Available: *http://www.anc.org.za*/show.php?id=3430 [Accessed 23 July 2015].

Reilly, E. T. 2013. *Business boot camp: management and leadership fundamentals that will see you successfully through your career.* New York: Amacom.

Tregoe, B. B., Zimmerman, J. W., Smith, R. A. & Tobia, P. M. 1989. *Vision in action putting winning strategy to work.* New York: Simon and Schuster.

Wilkins, D. & Carolin, G. 2013. *Leadership pure and simple: how transformative leaders create winning organisations.* New York: McGraw Hill.

Samuel, M, 2012. *Making Yourself Indispensible: The Power of Personal Accountability.* Penguin Group.

Endnotes

1 Coehlo, P. 2005. *Eleven minutes*. New York: Harper Perennial

2 Herrigel, E. 1953. *Zen in the art of archery*. [Online]. Available: http://www. ideologic.org/files/Eugen_Herrigel_-_Zen_in_the_Art_of_Archery.pdf [Accessed 23 July 2015].

3 Tolle, E. 1997. *The Power of Now: A Guide to Spiritual Enlightenment*. [Online]. Available: http://www.baytallaah.com/bookspdf/51.pdf [Accessed 23 July 2015].

4 ThinkExist.com. 2015. Maya Angelou quotes. [Online]. Available: http:// thinkexist.com/quotation/nothing_will_work_unless_you_do/215802.html [Accessed 23 July 2015].

5 Freud, A. 1946. *The ego and the mechanisms of defence*. New York: International Universities Press.

6 Confucius. 1870. 'The Doctrine of the Mean' in *The Chinese Classics* by James Legge. [Online]. Available: http://www.shsu.edu/~his_ncp/Confu.html [Accessed 23 July 2015].

7 Clance, P. R. & Imes, S. 1978. The Imposter Phenomenon in High Achieving Women: Dynamics and Therapeutic Intervention. *Psychotherapy Theory, Research, and Practice,* 15(3), 1-8, 15, 241 – 247.

8 Adizes, I. 1988. *Corporate Lifecycles: How and why corporations grow and die and what to do about it*. New York: Prentice Hall.

9 Collins, J. C. (2001). *Good to Great*. New York: Harper Collins.

10 BrainyQuote.com. 2015. William Jennings Bryan quotes. [Online]. Available: http://www.brainyquote.com/quotes/quotes/w/williamjen389006.html, [Accessed 23 July 2015].

11 Good Reads. 2015. Louise Hay Quotes. [Online]. Available: http://www. goodreads.com/author/quotes/74538.Louise_L_Hay?page=2 [Accessed 23 July 2015].

12 Frankl, V. E. 2004. *Man's search for meaning*. London: Random House.

13 Wikipedia. n.d. (a) St Augustine of Hippo. [Online]. Available at: https:// en.wikipedia.org/wiki/Augustine_of_Hippo. [Accessed 23 July 2015].

14 Wikipedia. n.d. (b) Marikana tragedy. 16 August 2012. [Online]. Available: https://en.wikipedia.org/wiki/Marikana_killings. [Accessed 23 July 2015].

15 Covey, S. R. 1989. *The 7 Habits of Highly Effective People*. New York: Simon and Schuster.

16 Concise Oxford English Dictionary. 2011. *Purpose*. New York: Oxford University Press

17 Jung, C. 2001. *Modern Man in Search of a Soul*. Abingdon: Routledge.

18 Taylor, S. 2012. *Back to Sanity. The healing of the Human Mind*. London: Hay House.

19 Frankl, V. E. 2004. *Man's search for meaning*. London: Random House.

20 Mail & Guardian. 25 February 2015. *Notes from the Design Indaba*. [Online]. Available: http://mg.co.za/article/2015-02-25-notes-from-the-design-indaba-conference-day-2 [Accessed 24 July 2015].

21 Ellsworth, R.E. 2002. *Leading with purpose: the new corporate realities*. Stanford: Stanford University Press.

22 The Economist. 2 June 2009. *Mission Statement*. [Online]. Available: http://www.economist.com/node/13766375. [Accessed 23 July 2015].

23 Worth, M. J. 2009. *Nonprofit Management: Principles and practice*. Los Angeles: SAGE Publications, Inc.

24 Munroe, M. 2003. *The Principles and Power of Vision*. New Kensington, PA: Whitaker House.

25 BrainyQuote.com. 2015. Walt Disney Quotes. [Online]. Available: http://www.brainyquote.com/quotes/quotes/w/waltdisney130027.html. [Accessed 23 July 2015].

26 Nelson, P. 1993. *There's a hole in my sidewalk: The romance of self-discovery*. Hillsboro, OR: Beyond Words Publications.

27 Wikiquote. n.d. Samuel Butler, Novelist. [Online]. Available: https://en.wikiquote.org/wiki/Samuel_Butler_(novelist). [Accessed 23 July 2015].

28 Ortberg, J. 2014. *If You Want to Walk on Water, You've Got to Get Out of the Boat*. Michigan: Zondervan.

29 Motivation for dreamers. n.d. Motivation Quotes. [Online]. Available: http://www.motivation-for-dreamers.com/motivation-quotes.html. [Accessed 23 July 2015].

30 Conant, D. & Norgaard, M. 2011. *Transforming everyday interactions into powerful leadership moments*. ASTD lecture. Orlando, Florida.

31 Fortune. 1997. *Killer strategies that make shareholders rich the top companies thrive, says our author a leading strategy guru by changing the rules of the game*. [Online]. Available: http://archive.fortune.com/magazines/fortune/fortune_archive/1997/06/23/228085/index.htm [Accessed 23 July 2015].

32 Mintzberg, H. 1992. *Five Ps for Strategy in The Strategy Process*. pp 12-19, H Mintzberg and JB Quinn eds., 1992. New York, NJ: Prentice-Hall International.

33 Nutt, P. C. 1984. Strategic planning network for non- profit organizations, *Strategic Management Journal*, 5(1), 57 – 75.

34 Mintzberg, H., Ahlstrand, B. & Lampel, J. 2005. *Strategy bites back*. London: Financial Times/Prentice Hall.

35 Bhide, A. 1999. *The origin and evolution of new businesses*. Oxford: Oxford University Press.

36 Sampler, J. L. 2014. *Bringing strategy back: How strategic shock absorbers make planning relevant in a world of constant change*. London: John Wiley & Sons.

37 O'Toole, J. 1996. *Leading change: the argument for values-based leadership.* New York: Ballantine Books.

38 Jansen Kraemer Jr., H. 2011. *The only true leadership is values-based leadership.* [Online]. Available: www.forbes.com/2011/04/26/values-based-leadership.html [Accessed 23 July 2015].

39 Lapin, D. 2012. *Lead by greatness.* [Online]. Available: http://www.leadbygreatness. com. [Accessed 24 July 2015].

40 Dean, K. W. 2008. *Values based leadership: how our personal values impact the workplace.* [Online]. Available: http://www.valuesbasedleadershipjournal.com/ issues/vol1issue1/deanphp. [Accessed 24 July 2015].

41 Sheehy, G. 2006. *Passages: Predictable crises of adult life.* New York: Random House LLC.

42 BrainyQuote.com. 2015. Peter Marshall Quotes. [Online]. Available: http://www.brainyquote.com/quotes/quotes/p/petermarsh382875. html#YQUYZs5TlvAEF0UE.99 [Accessed 23 July 2015].

43 Lichtenstein, S. 2012. *The role of values in leadership: how leader's values shape value creation.* [Online] Available: http://integralleadershipreview.com/6176-the-role-of-values-in-leadership-how-leaders-values-shape-value-creation/ [Accessed 23 July 2015].

44 Ernest, P. 2001. *The values journey.* Keynote address: ASTD International Conference and Expo (Florida, USA).

45 Waters, M. 2008. *Leadership values.* MBA Dissertation, Henley Management College/Brunel University.

46 Lichtenstein, S. 2005. *Strategy co-alignment: Strategic, executive values and organisational goal orientation and their impact on performance* (Doctoral dissertation, Henley Management College).

47 Drucker F. 2005. *Legacy advice from a wise man.* [Online]. Available: www. slideshare.net. [Accessed 23 July 2015].

48 Goshal, S. 2004. *The smell of the place.* Video of talk delivered at the World Economic Forum. [Online] Available: http://www.youtube.com/watch?v=UUddgE8rI0E [Accessed 21 March 2013].

49 Doran, G. T. 1981. There's a S.M.A.R.T. way to write management's goals and objectives. *Management Review, 70(11), 35-36.*

50 Johnson, B. 1996. *Polarity Management, Identifying and Managing Unolvable Problems.* Amherst, Mass: HRDPress Inc.

51 Sampler, J. L. 2014. *Bringing strategy back: How strategic shock absorbers make planning relevant in a world of constant change.* London: John Wiley & Sons.

52 Gottlieb, B.H. 1985. Social Support and the Study of Personal Relationships. *Journal of Social and Personal Relationships.* September, 1985 2: 351-375.

53 Brainy Quote. 2015. *Robert South Quotes.* [Online]. Available: http://www. brainyquote.com/quotes/quotes/r/robertsout186846.html. [Accessed 24 July 2015].

54 Nathan, G. 2004. *The franchise e-factor*. Brisbane: Franchise Relationships Institute.

55 Senge, P. 1990. *The fifth discipline: The art and practice of the learning organisation*. New York: Doubleday. 206.

56 Fineman, M. 1996. *The nature of visual illusion*. New York: Dover.

57 Search Quotes. 2015. Shannon Alder Quotes. [Online]. Available: http://www.searchquotes.com/quotation/Anger,_resentment_and_jealousy_doesn't_change_the_heart_of_others...it_only_changes_yours./324705/ [Accessed 24 July 2015].

58 Brainy Quotes. 2015a. Marcus Aurelius Quotes. [Online]. Available: http://www.brainyquote.com/quotes/quotes/m/marcusaure383110.html [Accessed 24 July 2015].

59 Brainy Quotes. 2015b. Ken Kesey Quotes. [Online]. Available: http://www.brainyquote.com/quotes/quotes/k/kenkesey380260.html [Accessed 24 July 2015].

60 Wisdom Quotes. 2015. James Kouzes and Barry Posner Quotes. [Online]. Available: http://www.wisdomquotes.com/quote/james-kouzes-and-barry-posner-1.html [Accessed 24 July 2015].

61 Monarth, H. 2014. The Irresistible Power of Storytelling as a Strategic Business Tool. *Harvard Business Review*. [Online]. Available: https://hbr.org/2014/03/the-irresistible-power-of-storytelling-as-a-strategic-business-tool/ [Accessed 24 July 2015].

62 Tichy, N. M. & Cohen, E. B. 1997. *The Leadership Engine: How Winning Companies Build Leaders at Every Level*. London: Harper Business.

63 Denning, S. 2001. *The Springboard: How Storytelling Ignites Action in Knowledge-era Organizations*. London: Butterworth-Heinemann.

64 Cranfield. 2015. *Storytelling is at the heart of leadership*. [Online]. Available: http://www.som.cranfield.ac.uk/som/dinamic-content/media/Praxis/Storytelling%20is%20at%20the%20heart%20of%20leadership.pdf [Accessed 24 July 2015].

65 Barakat, C. 2014. *The science of storytelling (infographic)*. [Online]. Available: www.adweek.com/socialtimes/science-storytelling-infographic/150296 [Accessed 24 July 2015]

66 Denning, S. 2001. *The Springboard: How Storytelling Ignites Action in Knowledge-era Organizations*. London: Butterworth-Heinemann.

67 Sampler, J. 2014. [See endnote 51]

68 Bach, R. 1970. Jonathan Livingston Seagull the Story. New York: Macmillan.

Index